30 WAYS TO IMPROVE YOUR GRADES

Harry Shaw

McGRAW-HILL BOOK COMPANY
New York St. Louis San Francisco London Paris Düsseldorf Tokyo Kuala Lumpur Mexico Montreal Panama São Paulo Sydney Toronto Johannesburg New Delhi Singapore

3456789FGFG8910321

Library of Congress Cataloging in Publication Data

Shaw, Harry
30 ways to improve your grades.

SUMMARY: Offers practical suggestions for budgeting time, increasing vocabulary, taking tests, and generally improving one's grades and educational foundations.
1. Study, Method of. 2. Thought and thinking.
[1. Study, Method of. 2. Learning and scholarship]
I. Title.
LB1049.S47 371.3'02812 75-42468
ISBN 0-07-056510-4

To the Reader

The book you hold in your hands is intended to help you improve your grades in whatever subjects you are studying. The suggestions it offers are as practical and pinpointed as I can make them. Some of the thirty steps to better grades are more important than others, but none is included that does not have a direct bearing upon study performance and resulting penalties or rewards.

Although the book attempts to be realistic in its no-nonsense advice, it is based upon firmly held ethical and moral beliefs. Nowhere does it suggest that you can get higher grades by:

Cheating
Taking only "easy" courses
Avoiding courses that require final examinations
Selecting teachers who have succumbed to student pressure for high grades
Electing only courses with pass–fail standings
Avoiding courses with "disliked" subject matter
Trying to intimidate teachers

Currying favor with teachers
Trying to substitute personality for performance

True, each of these practices is widespread. Each has "succeeded" in many instances. Each is morally wrong and eventually self-defeating.

This book is predicated on the conviction that a good education demands hard work and large amounts of constantly exerted self-discipline. In the pursuit of an education you can spend a lot of time learning very little unless you accept these two requirements and face them squarely. The easy, pleasant, merry road to learning unfailingly ends up on a detour to the dead end of ignorance. A good education rests precisely upon the foundations of straight thinking, intelligent reading, clear writing, and fluent speaking. It's possible to get high grades without any of these attainments, but not a solid education.

Genuine learning is a difficult, demanding enterprise. It is not an activity in which there are no rules and in which everyone wins. As a student, you have a moral obligation to study up to the realistically determined limits of your ability. In doing so, you will acquire the understanding and capabilities that will enrich your life and make you the thoughtful, informed, and responsible citizen you want and need to be.

H.S.

Contents

	To the Reader	v
1.	*Uncover Your Attitudes*	1
2.	*Change Some of Your Work Habits*	11
3.	*Take Care of Your Body and Brain*	19
4.	*Find Your Best Place and Time for Study*	29
5.	*Work within a Time Budget*	37
6.	*Try to Think Logically and Clearly*	45
7.	*Understand What You Read*	57
8.	*Get Rid of Bad Reading Habits*	65
9.	*Train Your Memory to Commit Itself*	70
10.	*Learn to Listen While Listening to Learn*	77
11.	*Put into Your Own Words What You Read and Hear*	83
12.	*Take Notes in Précis Form*	91
13.	*View and Then Review*	98
14.	*Learn to Talk with People*	104
15.	*Learn to Talk to People*	108

16. *Say It Right* 116
17. *Make Friends with Your Dictionary* 122
18. *Increase Your Vocabulary* 133
19. *Say Exactly What You Mean* 141
20. *Don't Be a Rubber Stamp* 158
21. *Get Rid of Deadwood* 166
22. *Take Seven Steps to Better Sentences* 172
23. *Spell It Right* 181
24. *Punctuate It Right* 193
25. *Divide and Conquer* 198
26. *Discover Your Library* 205
27. *Take Three Steps to Better Papers and Reports* 217
28. *Write Legibly* 225
29. *Revise and Proofread Everything You Write* 231
30. *Improve Your Test-taking Methods* 237

30
WAYS TO IMPROVE YOUR GRADES

1

Uncover Your Attitudes

Your first step toward better grades should be to find out—as honestly, specifically, and fully as you can—how you really feel about the process of learning.

Is school a bore? Is study a waste of time? Do you like some subjects and hate others? Do you resent the hours you spend in learning, feeling they could be better spent? Do you fail to see how school is really helpful in increasing your chances for success in doing or achieving whatever you most want? Is it a pleasure? Do you have fun learning new things? Is it exciting to realize that you are growing in mind and understanding?

Honest answers to these questions will help you understand why your performance is poor, average, or excellent. You know, don't you, that you are unlikely to get a role in a play unless you are genuinely interested in dramatics and eager to be chosen for a part? You know that interest, dedication, and willingness to rehearse may outweigh other considerations, including natural ability to act. You realize that your chances for making an athletic team depend on willingness and eagerness to practice and learn as well as on physical ability. You know that everything you have learned to do was influenced, consciously or unconsciously, by how much you wanted to do it: dancing, painting, cooking, sewing, needlework, swimming, singing, playing a musical instrument, skating, or whatever.

The skills you can attain in any activity, including those just mentioned, are affected by your desire, interest, and willingness to try. If you want to do any activity well, you are willing to pay the necessary price in time and effort. If you aren't, your success will be limited. You will start on one, grow bored or discouraged, and say "Oh, I never really wanted to learn to dance"—or ski or play basketball or jump rope.

Study, like any other worthwhile activity, requires work. It requires *hard* work. Nearly 2500 years ago, Euclid, the great Greek educator, wrote that there is no "royal road" to geometry. No royal road has ever been found to the mastery of that mathematical science or any other branch of learning. Millions of people think study is pleasurable, rewarding, and even exciting—but no one has ever found it "easy." Do not expect to be the first to make that discovery.

"But," you say, "I really do wish to learn." Good! But remember that *wish* and *will* differ widely. Nearly everyone *wishes* to learn something or other, but a wish is only a form of "desire" or "longing." The only way for you or me or anyone to make a wish come true is to dig in, to apply ourselves to the task at hand. If you want to achieve greater success in learning you must find out what's the matter with your studying and then make up your mind to do something about it. Nearly a century ago, an American author, Elbert Hubbard, wrote:

> It is not book learning young men need, nor instruction about this and that, but a stiffening of the vertebrae which will cause them to . . . act promptly, to concentrate their energies, to do a thing.

Being interested is a necessity for real success in whatever you want to do. As a student, you have a responsibility to be or to become interested in studying. No one can be interested for you. Interest cannot be inherited or produced by some magic formula. Teachers cannot arouse your interest unless you want them to. Interest comes solely from your desire to be involved and your willingness to make an effort to "get with it."

If you lack interest in every subject you are supposed to be studying, your problem is really serious. Short of quitting entirely, you should try to uncover the reasons for your lack of interest. A frank talk with a teacher, guidance counselor, or some other person might help. If a conscientious effort to find reasons fails completely, you must accept the fact that study for you may be an impossibility or, at best, an activity slated for failure and disappointment.

For nearly everyone, however, some subjects have a natural interest; others seem boring or difficult. These differing attitudes apply to all the activities we engage in, in school or out. Some of the things you do regularly seem to please, comfort, excite, or reward. Others are routinely dull and uninspiring. It is sensible to conclude that some studies will absorb and entertain you and some will not. No one is expected to have a real interest in every subject studied any more than one is required to exhibit interest in every activity engaged in throughout the day.

In getting a well-rounded education, you will have to perform many tasks that don't appeal to you. The poet and essayist T. S. Eliot once said, "No one can become really educated without having pursued some study in which he took no interest—for it is a part of education to learn to interest ourselves in subjects for which we have no aptitude."

The surest way to develop interest in a subject is to learn something about it. Surely you have met someone who didn't appeal at all, but discovered that as you came to know him or her better your interest increased. You may have wound up liking or disliking that person, but you were no longer uninterested. You can and should make the same discovery about every subject you are studying. Learning even a little about a foreign language, or math, or history, or any other discipline that may seem uninteresting is an important first step toward interest, regardless of whether you come to like or detest that subject. It's impossible to learn to swim without getting your feet wet.

Once you have acquired even a slight interest in some subject, you will begin to see how and why it may be helpful to you. This knowledge will provide motivation for continuing to study it. Your motive in certain courses may be no greater than to pass them because they are required for a certificate or diploma. This is hardly an inspired or lofty urge, but it is undeniably practical. Your awakening interest in some subject, however, may move you toward a realization that it will have dollars-and-cents value in later life. (And don't make the mistake of thinking that only such courses as computer sciences and chemistry have monetary potentials. Your earning power in later life may depend heavily on the ideas you have, the extent of your vocabulary, your ability to read, and your facility in communicating with others orally or in writing.)

No matter what your motivation, your determination to master a subject will become stronger when you discover sound reasons for studying it. If you can't supply reasons on your own, look for them elsewhere. Your teacher and other students in your classes can help you recognize them.

Genuine success in studying is impossible without a substantial degree of interest and motivation. Your own experience in many activities has proved that when you become sufficiently interested in something to exert real effort for a real reason, your success is great or satisfactory—or at least more than you once thought possible.

Your attitude toward study depends heavily on interest and

motivation. For that matter, your attitude toward anything determines your reaction to it. Your entire life will be controlled by how you feel about such matters as work, money, love, food, marriage, health, and goals in living. Your attitudes may be wise or unwise, healthy or unhealthy, reasonable or illogical. No matter what they are, neither you nor I can escape the sure knowledge that how we think and feel determines the course of our lives. Shakespeare's Hamlet remarked, "There is nothing either good or bad but thinking makes it so." Your opinion that school is "good" or "bad" depends upon your attitude toward work and life. And you alone are responsible for that attitude.

Without regard for environment and heredity, the attitudes most directly affecting school, college, and adult study involve discipline, teachers, fellow students, and books. Let's consider each in turn.

Discipline

The institution in which you are studying may be strictly regimented, with numerous rules and regulations. It may be a permissive one in which conduct is loosely supervised. No matter. Whether your school is strict or lenient, sooner or later life will impose its own disciplines of many kinds. A part of education involves learning to live with an order and restraint that are self-willed or imposed by law or custom.

If you cannot live with the discipline imposed by your institution, you should change schools or drop out entirely. This statement does not imply that you should become a slave and knuckle under to all disciplinary demands. If certain rules and requirements don't make sense, you have a right to try to get them changed. Nor does the statement mean that you must comply with every governing direction any more than every citizen should always obey every law on the statute books. It does mean that your behavior should be positive, not negative. It does suggest that dislike for regulations and impatience with rules should not be allowed to upset, torment, or distract you from the central purpose of fitting into your environment and concentrating on your main job, learning.

In the last fifty years, educational institutions have become less regimented than they were. Freedom of thought and action are not merely tolerated but encouraged. And yet the necessity for self-discipline, for sticking to the job at hand, has not lessened. Actually, as competition for grades has increased, so has the demand for self-control. In seeking better grades, you will have to force yourself to perform tasks you don't like. You will need to make yourself conform, at least outwardly, to the requirements of your school relating to behavior and accomplishment. As interest and motivation grow, you may find it a relief to get with the discipline imposed by yourself and others. In short, your attitude toward discipline should be constructive, not self-defeating.

Teachers

One reason for failure is the tendency to think that some or all teachers are enemies, not friends. Some students, both young and old, consider teachers demanding, unsympathetic, even vicious. In any profession—law, dentistry, medicine, preaching, engineering, teaching—some practitioners fall short in many ways. There is no proof that the percentage of incompetent and sadistic teachers is any higher than that of professionals in other learned occupations. In fact, most teachers (admittedly not all) are dedicated, knowledgeable, earnest men and women who genuinely want their students to succeed.

Your attitude toward teachers may influence your grades more than you realize. It is difficult to work for someone whom you dislike or you think dislikes you. It is discouraging to believe that no matter how hard or well you work, your teacher will not give you proper credit. It is destructive to become so "tuned out" that you "turn off."

It should help to remember that every teacher is first a person and second a teacher. Being human, teachers have their strengths and weaknesses, just as students do. They have their mannerisms and opinions, their virtues and faults, just as students do. They have their good days and their bad days, just as students do. Most of the time, teachers are earnestly dedicated to imparting knowledge to their students about subjects they believe important. But it is wise to look upon them as men and women first and members of a learned profession second.

You do not have to be a favor-seeker, teacher's pet, or hypocrite when you make an effort to understand your instructors. Watching teachers in action, listening, asking questions, and talking to them outside classroom and laboratory may radically change your attitude toward them and the subjects they teach. Getting to know teachers better will prove that they are not ogres or bores, that what they teach may be important to you as well as to them, and that they will readily exhibit as much interest in you as you do in them. Isn't it only human to expect teachers to appear bored, indifferent, unhelpful, and sarcastic when you yourself are inattentive, restless, and rude?

Fellow Students

Unless you are a politician, there's no reason for you to try to get to know all your classmates or to curry favor with them. Even so, if you consistently ignore all of them, you may be neglecting an important means of furthering your education.

Look at it this way. Each of your classmates is an individual with a background somewhat different from yours. Each knows things you don't. You share a common problem with each: passing a course. Every one of them can and does affect your attitude toward a particular class and learning in general.

Much of your education is obtained outside the classroom. Your classmates contribute heavily to that education. What you learn from them may be helpful or harmful, but either way it's important. Two great benefits of the entire process of schooling are learning to get along with others and sharing common experiences.

Becoming friends with a classmate has altered the attitude of many a student toward school and study. If you feel that none of your classmates is worth knowing, you are not likely to go to school every day in a happy frame of mind. But if there is one person or more among your classmates whom you get to know and with whom you can share ideas, plans, time, and activities, hours in school will take on new meaning and become less monotonous.

A suggestion: Give some hard thought to the person or group among your classmates with whom you most associate. Are he, she, or they a good or bad influence? Does this individual or group help or hinder you in your reach for better grades? Supply your own answer, but make it an honest one. And remember this: Countless students have discovered their outlooks, attitudes, and grades changing as they deepened their friendships with classmates. In every class you are taking, someone can help you, someone can harm you. Why not stay away from those students who have a "losing" attitude? Why not stick with the winners? Doing just this is more sensible than it is snobbish.

Books

Many tools are used to provide you with an education: lectures, classroom sessions, learning centers, laboratories, and the like. All are significant and have their place, but the most centrally important learning tool of all is books. How you feel about books probably reflects much of your attitude toward all formal education. If, in general, you like books, you have a great advantage. If you don't like books, if you fear or distrust them, face up to the fact that nearly all forms of education (including those provided by trade schools, technical institutes, secretarial schools, agricultural centers) depend to some extent on books.

Now, you cannot force yourself to like books any more than you can make yourself fall in love with someone. But you can change your attitudes toward books if you give them some attention and gradually alter your perspectives about them. Consider these points:

1. *No one likes all books and probably no one (meaning you) dislikes every kind of book.*

Don't make the mistake of thinking that you "hate" books just because some of your textbooks and other required reading don't appeal to you. A major purpose of education is elevating your tastes so that you come, however slowly, to realize that your reading diet need not be restricted to comics, joke books, slick magazines, and love stories. Another purpose of schooling is to get you to see that many kinds of books are both helpful and enjoyable. Figure out your present attitude toward books and slowly attempt to rectify it if it reflects fear or distaste.

2. *Books are here to stay.*

In time, it may be possible to acquire a good general education without the use of books. That time has not arrived. People out of school who claim they don't read books are conning themselves. Merchants read books on retailing or go bankrupt. Housewives read cookbooks. Physicians read medical tomes. Everyone who is literate is directly affected by books of some kind; they are inescapable. You may as well decide right now that books will continue to be necessities and that it is wise to decide if "you can't lick 'em, join 'em." Arriving at this decision will not necessarily increase your liking for books, but it will cause you to appreciate their importance.

3. *Books are a symbol of civilization.*

Through books preserved in all the libraries of the world we can benefit from what wise persons of many times, races, and nations have said and thought and done. You may lack respect for books, but think what our world would be like if we could not build on the wisdom and experience of the past. You may never learn to revere books, but the sooner you come to respect them, the sooner your interest in learning will increase and thus strengthen your motivation to achieve better grades.

No one has better expressed the importance of books than an American writer, Clarence Day:

> The world of books is the most remarkable creation of man. Nothing else that he builds ever lasts. Monuments fall, nations perish, civilizations grow old and die out, and after an era of darkness new races build others. But in the world of books are volumes that have seen this happen again and again and yet live on, still young, still as fresh as the day they were written, still telling men's hearts of the hearts of men centuries dead.

2

Change Some of Your Work Habits

" 'Habit a second nature! Habit is ten times nature,' the Duke of Wellington is said to have exclaimed." Thus begins an essay by William James, this country's famous pioneer psychologist. No more true or helpful words have ever been written about habit and nature.

Nature may be defined as the particular combination of qualities, instincts, and inborn tendencies that control conduct. We say of someone that he or she is "by nature" a shy or modest or outspoken person; that he is studious or cruel, by nature, or that she is careless or thoughtful. By *second nature* is meant those acquired tendencies or habits so deeply ingrained in one's character that they seem automatic. Thus we say of someone that it is "second nature" for her to try to help others or that a love of sports is "second nature" to him.

And what is *habit*? It is usually thought of as "a customary practice," "a dominant or regular disposition or tendency." We say that someone has formed the habit of saving money, or taking daily baths, or sleeping ten hours in every twenty-four. Everyone, no matter how young or old, has formed many habits. Actually, everyone's life is shaped and directed by the habits he or she has formed. James refers to habits as "the enormous flywheel of society." Chaos would result if most people had not formed the habits of obeying traffic regulations, observing legal restrictions, meeting their obligations, and living generally orderly lives.

As a member of the human race, you are a mass of habits. Some of these habits may be considered good, some bad. Since this book is not primarily concerned with ethics and morals, it will not label which is which. But this chapter *is* directly concerned with habits that promote effective study and with habits that interfere with study and result in grades lower than you wish and need.

As if you didn't already know them, members of your family, friends, acquaintances, and teachers have freely and regularly pointed out "bad" habits you have acquired. You have a good idea of what these habits are. You'd like to get rid of them. But can you? How? If it's your "nature" to do the kind of studying that results in low grades, if it's "second nature" to play rather than work, to relax rather than exert yourself, to expect low grades as a matter of course, how can you develop habits ten times stronger than either nature or second nature?

In starting to rid yourself of bad study habits, don't try to tackle all of them at once. Attempting to drop habits wholesale is as silly as trying to develop a new personality overnight. (But it won't hurt to remember that your personality is largely the direct result, the cumulative total, of your habits—good ones, bad ones, indifferent ones.) Take on your bad habits one at a time and expect no miracles.

"Wait a minute," you say. "My habits are so fixed that I couldn't change them no matter how much I want to." This is an understandable response, but it's inaccurate. You *can* change habits. Start with only one habit and make it an easy or unimportant one. For example, whether you are aware of it or not, you habitually insert first your left or right leg into slacks you are putting on. Keep a simple chart, alternating days (or times) for starting with your left and right legs. Such an exercise is not meaningless, although it seems unimportant. Your success in breaking this trivial habit will *prove* to yourself that you *can* break a habit.

Then practice with other "easy" and "unimportant" habits: which shoe you put on first, whether you start with upper or lower (or front or back) teeth when brushing them, what you eat for breakfast, what part of your body you soap first when taking a shower, or any of a hundred other minor practices that are firmly fixed as habits, however unaware you may be of them.

Having proved to yourself and others that you can break a habit, always keep in mind that any habit discarded must be replaced. All nature, including yours and mine, abhors a vacuum. If, for instance, you have a habit of speaking too rapidly, you don't break it by saying nothing. Instead of speaking fast you resort to slow and deliberate speech. If you are in the habit of making an instant response to anything addressed to you, form a new habit of counting silently to five or ten before replying. You don't dehydrate yourself if you decide to break the habit of numerous soft drinks; you drink enough other liquids to keep you going.

In summary: (1) tackle habits one at a time, (2) start with easy, "harmless" habits, (3) always replace one habit with another.

As William James points out in his essay, the "great thing in all education" is to "make our nervous system our ally instead of our enemy." To accomplish this aim, James insists that "we must make automatic and habitual as many useful actions as we can." He suggests that the more details of our lives we can leave in "the custody of automatism," the freer we will be to settle down to what he calls "proper work." No one is more miserable than the person for whom nothing is a fixed habit except that of indecision, of wondering whether he should do this or that—take a nap or a walk, wear this or that clothing, eat a snack, or whatever is needed to fill time or accomplish something.

Fixed, suitable, and regular habits of study can contribute much to making our nervous systems our aids and companions, not our adversaries.

In seeking to form a new habit as a replacement for an old one, follow these suggestions, unless you have something better to offer:

1. *Start work on the new habit with determination to succeed.*

If you begin halfheartedly, thinking you will fail, you will. If you develop your resolution with every aid you can think of, you will probably succeed. Keep away from persons, places, and activities that may weaken your resolve. (A person trying to quit drinking alcohol should not eat lunch in a bar.) Put yourself in situations and conditions that will encourage the "new way" you want to develop. (Unplug the TV or radio while you're trying to study.)

2. *Never let occur an exception to the new habit.*

Continuity is essential. It's impossible to form a new habit if you allow slips or breaks to occur. (If you are forming the habit of studying for a solid hour five nights a week, don't ever say "Just this once I'll listen to a record or tape for a few minutes.") As James insists, each lapse in forming a new habit is like dropping a ball of yarn that one is winding up. One slip undoes more than many turns will rewind. Every gain on the "wrong" side undoes the effect of several gains on the "right" side.

A comforting thought is that as you proceed with forming a new habit, the task gets easier. It will be difficult at first to change an old pattern and adopt a new one, but repeated efforts will cause the old habit to fade and the new one to become easier and more natural. Shakespeare's Hamlet makes this point clearly when he urges his mother not to go to bed with her new husband:

> . . . Refrain tonight
> And that shall lend a kind of easiness
> To the next abstinence; the next more easy;
> For use can almost change the stamp of nature
> And either master the devil or throw him out.

The comments in this chapter, which owes much to James' *Principles of Psychology*, can best be clarified by this paragraph from the chapter entitled "Habit":

> The hell to be endured hereafter, of which theology tells us, is no worse than the hell we make for ourselves in this world by habitually fashioning our characters in the wrong way. Could the young but realize how soon they will become mere walking bundles of habits, they would give more heed to their conduct while in the plastic state. We are spinning our own fates, good or evil, and never to be undone. Every smallest stroke of virtue or of vice leaves its never so little scar. The drunken Rip Van Winkle . . . excuses himself for every fresh dereliction by saying, "I won't count this time." Well, he may not count it and a kind Heaven may not count it; but it is being counted nonetheless. Down among his nerve cells and fibres, the molecules are counting it, registering and storing it up to be used against him when the next temptation comes. Nothing we ever do, in strict scientific literalness, is wiped out. . . . As we become drunkards by so many separate drinks, so we become saints in the moral, and authorities and experts in the practical and scientific spheres, by so many separate acts and hours of work. Let no youth have any anxiety about the upshot of his education. If he keeps faithfully busy each hour of the working day, he may safely leave the final result to itself. He can with perfect certainty count on waking up some fine morning to find himself one of the competent ones of his generation.

Each reader will have to determine what his bad study habits are and which of them, if any, he or she wants to change. If you do decide to make some changes and are successful in doing so, you will have taken a major step toward greater satisfaction in all your study. And a part of that satisfaction will come from the higher grades you will begin receiving.

What follows is a list of habits that have proved useful and effective for millions of students. Probably no one who ever lived has followed all of them or is capable of doing so, because they constitute what might be called a "counsel of perfection." But balance your work habits against these. Select the ones you wish to work on. In doing so, follow the suggestions offered in preceding paragraphs. Don't set yourself impossible tasks. Don't get discouraged by failures. Keep on keeping on. Big shots are little shots who kept on shooting.

IN PREPARING FOR CLASS

1. Make working conditions as suitable as possible
2. Have all study materials immediately at hand
3. Stay awake; don't daydream
4. Determine work quotas in advance
5. Interrupt study only with short breaks
6. Waste no time
7. Stay with it; don't doodle or dawdle

IN CLASSROOM AND LABORATORY

1. Arrive with necessary equipment: books, pencils, notebooks
2. Listen carefully to the teacher and fellow students
3. Sit or stand erect; keep alert
4. Enter into class discussions
5. Ask questions when puzzled

6. Make notes in your own words
7. Write down assignments in a notebook or assignment book
8. Keep lists of grades, missed assignments, and the like
9. Relate what you hear and do to what you already know
10. Briefly review immediately after class the results of every session

IN LIBRARY AND STUDY HALL

1. Have all needed study gear with you
2. Know precisely what you want to accomplish
3. Get down to work right away
4. Block out disrupting noise and movement
5. Don't distract others
6. Take careful, full, legible notes
7. At the end of each session, review what you have learned

OUTSIDE SCHOOL

1. Keep yourself in good physical shape: sleep, exercise, diet, and so on
2. Do some reading every day: newspapers, magazines, unassigned books
3. Talk with others on significant topics
4. Really listen to people who might broaden your knowledge
5. Ask thought-provoking questions of others: parents, teachers, friends, fellow employees, employers
6. Budget your time: sleep, study, chores
7. Get some needed relaxation every day

At the risk of appearing moralistic, it might be suggested that some teachers tend to grade student performance on grounds other than what students know and can communicate. Such matters as appearance, manners, and general conduct often have an impact on grades. Teachers, or most of them anyway, like to have their students

1. Take pride in their work
2. Act courteously in class and out
3. Reveal self-discipline
4. Show respect for others
5. Respect school property
6. Assume responsibility
7. Cooperate with others

What your attitudes and habits are in these matters is a main concern of this book. Each of them is worth examination and, if necessary, remedial steps.

Study involves (1) the development of mental habits and (2) the organization of one's will toward exercising one's mind. It is simpler to say that your life as a student is determined and directed by your attitudes, habits, and practices. What has been said about *attitudes* and *habits* should be sufficient to get you started on the specific *practices* discussed in the remainder of this book. Yet your reaction to each of the following twenty-eight steps, your success or failure with them, will rest squarely on your attitudes about them and the habits you have formed and are forming.

3

Take Care of Your Body and Brain

A chapter on personal care in a book about improving grades may seem unnecessary. You have long since become bored with advice about taking care of yourself, with admonitions about cleanliness, brushing teeth, and wearing suitable clothing. This chapter is not so much about hygiene as a reminder that effective study depends heavily on the state of one's brain and body. Each of us knows something about our brains and bodies, but each of us tends to neglect them for what we consider more important matters.

Your mind—however you define this process or element that feels, thinks, perceives, wills, and judges—is wholly dependent upon your brain. The brain is an actual organ (which the mind is not); it is that part of the central nervous system enclosed in the cranium. The brain, in turn, is dependent upon other organs of the body for its nurture, care, and development. The Latin phrase *mens sana in corpore sano* (a sound mind in a sound body) has been a practical, sensible maxim for more than 2000 years.

Your list and mine of our most prized possessions would

differ, but brain and body should rank high on anyone's inventory. Each is a fine and delicate mechanism. Each deserves care and attention. And each of us occasionally or regularly abuses his body and his brain. Who among us does not sometimes ignore the soundest advice ever given for comfortable, constructive living: "Never get tired, never get hungry, never get bored"?

True, situations that cause us to overwork these mutually dependent mechanisms of body and brain do arise. We can, and do, stretch ourselves to attempt extraordinary tasks. We bully our wills into doing more than we should. In Rudyard Kipling's poem "If" these lines occur:

> . . . force your heart and nerve and sinew
> To serve your turn long after they are gone,
> And so hold on when there is nothing in you
> Except the Will which says to them "Hold on."

One's heart and nerve and sinew may need to be overtaxed on rare occasions, but the practice should not become chronic. Better grades are likely to escape everyone who consistently abuses his body and brain. A hard, consistent worker is quite different from an overanxious, exhausted drudge.

If in the past you have greatly overtaxed your body and brain, you should see a physician, psychologist, neurosurgeon, or psychiatrist. If brain and body have been abused but not permanently damaged, you can start to repair them by proper attention to their five primary needs: proper diet, exercise, sleep, relaxation, and recreation.

Diet

Scientists agree that there is no such thing as brain food, but they also agree that one's body and brain are built from what is put into them.

If you are typical, you think that you follow a "normal" or "balanced" diet. Rarely if ever are you really hungry. You eat two, three, or more meals a day and probably worry more about overeating than proper eating. Most dietitians and other nutritional experts, however, know that there is no such thing as a normal diet, that food intake varies enormously in quantity and quality from person to person, and that large numbers of people following a so-called balanced diet actually suffer from malnutrition and related deficiency diseases. It is a rare institutional cafeteria or dining room that consistently provides items regularly needed in a good diet. It is a rare eater in such places who usually selects those items most needed by his body and brain. It is a rare home diet that, no matter how bountiful and even luxurious, is not often deficient in food essentials.

What you should eat is a matter for nutritional experts to decide. But what you should not eat is a matter of common sense. Perhaps it would be more accurate to say that your body will usually tell you what not to overeat. The author is as fond of "dead" foods as anyone reading this book: cake, soft drinks, candy, and all coin-machine delights. For several months, as a graduate student, he regularly arose late and ate a hurried "breakfast" from a vending machine consisting of peanut-butter–smeared crackers and a soft drink. He knew but ignored the needs of his body and brain for a better breakfast. He knew but often overlooked their needs during the day for eggs, milk, fruit, vegetables, and other body-building and brain-nourishing produce.

If you wish to form the habit of keeping your body and brain fit to engage in the rigorous study practices outlined in this book, consider these suggestions:

1. No matter how many snacks you indulge in during the day, try to consume at least one balanced meal: vegetables (not overcooked); fresh meat, poultry, or fish; fresh fruit; and some farm or dairy products such as milk and eggs.

2. Do not eat a heavy meal just before an important test

or examination. Overeating may make you sluggish or sleepy. Remember that a football team eats a carefully selected and prepared meal hours before a game. A stiff quiz requires as much mental exertion as a game demands in physical output.

3. Avoid the overuse of stimulants. The suggestion is practical, not moral. The use of stimulants in moderation may not be unwise, but nearly everyone has a tendency to overindulge. Many persons ingest more caffeine than their bodies can safely absorb by drinking excessive amounts of coffee, tea, and cola preparations. Caffeine can be a harmless and even helpful stimulant, but excessive amounts cause it to lose its effectiveness and even result in digestive ailments. Remember, too, that coffee, tea, and soft drinks have a diuretic effect; pushed for time in an examination, you will regret having to trek to a bathroom for relief.

4. Be careful with sedatives and "pep" pills. Alcohol and nicotine are sedatives, not stimulants as they are often thought to be. A sedative is hardly something to be overindulged in when strenuous mental activity and exertion are involved. Whatever your habits concerning alcohol and cigarettes—and these are your business—think of them as sedatives, products designed to soothe and calm. If you indulge in either, try to be moderate. No one, alcoholics and "nicotine fiends" included, can sensibly defend their excessive use.

Most persons, physicians and nurses among them, consider "pep" pills the resource of foolish or stupid people. If a licensed medical practitioner prescribes them, that's his business and yours. But no matter how much amphetamines may spur you on for a time, they tend to build up a "fatigue debt." They will drive you ahead during long hours of study but may let you down when you most need to exhibit the results of that study during a test. All mood changers are more likely to affect your judgment and cause you to feel intoxicated than to increase your mental agility and sharpen your memory.

Exercise

Exercise is bodily or mental exertion for training and improving the mind and body. Most of this book deals with mental effort; these few paragraphs discuss activities designed to improve the body that houses the mind.

Only a few hundred years ago, our ancestors spent most of their waking hours in physical pursuits—fishing, trapping, and hunting animals. In but a few centuries we have largely become persons spending most of our time in houses, stores, factories, offices, and schools. Unless we plan for and engage in physical exertion, we tend to become soft, flabby, and dull. A mind can be sounder than the body that houses it, but the ideal is still *mens sana in corpore sano*. Sensibly planned exercise makes one feel better physically and sharply increases ability to think, study, and perform in the classroom.

If you resolve to exercise your body regularly as one means of improving your mind, consider:

1. *Physical exertion is not necessarily exercise.*

You may think you get exercise running for a bus, doing housework, washing clothes, clerking in a store, or walking through halls or across a campus. Not so. Such exertion may tire you, but it is not likely to tone up your muscles or clear your mind. Proper exercise makes you breathe more deeply, causes you to perspire, and leaves you feeling refreshed.

2. *Good exercise is good fun.*

You may dislike what you call exercise because it bores you. Each of us knows from experience that doing calisthenics or working alone in a gym can be tedious. If such exertion is just this for you, then seek some exercise that is enjoyable. If walking seems dull, find a walking companion. Try to develop your skill at some active sport. Not everyone wants to play football or basketball; how about swimming or badminton or jogging or tennis or golf or archery or some form of dancing? A physical education teacher or athletic coach can provide useful suggestions. Don't exercise if doing so bores you. Find some exercise that pleases, relaxes, and refreshes you.

3. *Use common sense in exercising.*

If you have gone without exercise for a long time, start slowly. Overexertion will result in stiff muscles, weariness, and a sore back or legs. As you work into activity, you can gradually increase the time and physical energy expended.

4. *Exercise is a means, not an end in itself.*

Even athletes in school on scholarships should never forget (and some seem to) that they are first students and second performing artists. As a student, your primary aim should not be to build up bulging muscles, make an athletic team, or become Mr. or Miss America. It should be to improve your muscle tone, digestion, and circulation so that these systems can more adequately serve your brain—which is dependent upon them. Sensible, regular exercise will help you think, study, and perform better than perhaps you ever have before.

Sleep

The amount of sleep people need is debatable. Some persons claim to get by with three hours' sleep in every twenty-four. Others insist that they need nine or ten hours every night. The truth is that most of us feel a need for the amount of sleep we have formed the habit of getting. On occasion, we can keep going for several days with practically no sleep. At other times, we delight in sleeping round the clock.

Experts generally agree that all but exceptional people require from seven to nine hours' sleep in every twenty-four, no more and no less. Perhaps you are like the author: too little sleep leaves him jumpy, irritable, and nervous; too much makes him drowsy, dull, and phlegmatic. Experiment to find out what amount of sleep enables you to function best and then try to get that amount regularly.

Mull over what follows about sleep. Apply it to yourself. But please do not ignore it because it has an important bearing upon your quest for better grades.

1. *Nothing should be allowed to interfere with proper sleep.*

You may, for example, think that you are obligated to study most or all of the night before an important exam. You say "I have much to cover and no other time for it." It would make more sense to get a good night's sleep, regardless of how much is left undone. Solid sleep that restores mind and body will help you more in the classroom or examination hall than hours of last-minute, frantic cramming. If you still do badly on the test, you can resolve to change your study habits before another test comes along. Instead of spending your weekends in the sack, you will do some ahead-of-time reviewing (see Chapter 13). Instead of fooling away afternoons in idle chatter or wasted activity, you will budget your time (see Chapter 5). Whatever you do, remember that your body and brain are engines that demand regular and sufficient rest.

2. *Your sleep schedule is based on habit.*

Despite the problems you may have in getting to sleep, getting enough sleep, or getting too much sleep, solutions are available. If, for instance, you are accustomed to staying up until well after midnight, you are likely to turn and toss if you pop into the feathers at 10:00 or 11:00 P.M. Try this scheme: if you usually go to bed at 1:00 A.M., try for a week to turn in at 12:30. By the end of a week (or longer if necessary) you will have acquired the habit of sleeping an additional half-hour. Then for a week or two, try getting to bed at midnight. By tapering off over a period of weeks you can alter your sleep patterns as much as you wish.

Millions of people have adjusted their sleeping schedules by forming new habits. Milkmen get their sleep at odd hours. So do firemen, policemen, hospital nurses, cleaning women, family doctors, garbage collectors, and countless others with topsy-turvy time schedules. You can train your body just as you would that of any other animal.

3. *Try to relax before going to bed.*

It's difficult to go to sleep promptly when your mind is still occupied with serious matters, including study, heavy reading, and prolonged thought. For a half-hour before "blackout" time, listen to some quiet music, read a light book or magazine article or story, or talk with someone about commonplace affairs. If you are an especially anxious-for-sleep person, try a warm bath, a glass of milk, a cup of cocoa, or even a mild sedative. (Remember that warm drinks and sedatives of whatever kind tend to become crutches and should be given up as soon as you no longer need them.)

Relaxing one's mind by relaxing one's muscles can also help induce sleep. With a little practice you can learn to relax muscle-groups of the face, the arms, the mouth, the legs. Let them go limp and even sag.

After experimenting, you will discover what amount of sleep you need each night to restore body and brain to maximum efficiency. Having arrived at a schedule right for you, stay with it. Let nothing interfere with it during your work week.

Relaxation and Recreation

Medical research has proved the truth of the old saw that "all work and no play makes Jack a dull boy" and Jill a dull girl. Your body and brain require relaxation and recreation just as they need proper nutrition, exercise, and sleep. If they seem sensible and feasible, follow these suggestions for relaxing and recreating yourself:

1. *Interrupt your studying now and then.*

You may be able to concentrate on a textbook hour after hour, but most of us feel our attention slipping, our determination weakening, after a certain time. When this occurs, it is neither weak-willed nor thoughtless to stop studying. A five- or ten-minute break every hour can be helpful. (If you were in the Army on a route march, this is exactly what would be ordered.) Get up from your chair and stretch. Walk around a bit. Play a favorite record or tape. Wash your face and hands, especially your eyes. Make a *short* telephone call. Don't prolong these rest intervals; get back to work. Such breaks are calculated to help you resume studying with renewed vigor and increased understanding.

2. *Plan your recreation to suit individual needs.*

Recreation means refreshment through some pastime, agreeable exercise, diversion, or entertainment. If television refreshes you, watch it occasionally; if it bores you, let it alone. If casual conversation stimulates you, engage in it. If it seems a mind-wearying bore, avoid it. If you like parties, dates, and dances because they relax you, go to as many (or have as many) as you can afford in time and money. If they don't refresh, give them up. Carefully analyze just which spectator sports, hobbies, games, and other diversions improve your body and frame of mind. Engage in them for help; stay away from those that contribute little or nothing.

Try every day to budget your time (see Chapter 5) to allow for some recreation and relaxation. But remember that too much of either is ruinous to progress as a student. Too little will keep you bored and discontented. The right amount of the right kinds (for you) will improve your studying and the grades you get for it.

In summary, never forget that one's body is "fearfully and wonderfully made" and that one's brain is a fine and delicate instrument. Neither should be abused. Neither should be neglected. Neither should be driven too hard or allowed to stagnate. Care for them as your most prized possessions, for that is precisely what they are.

4

Find Your Best Place and Time for Study

Where and when you study may be more important considerations than you realize. Some people can concentrate on what they're doing regardless of surroundings and the time of day or night. Most of us, however, seem to work best at certain times and in certain places. Discovering the conditions and time periods that contribute to your efficiency is an important step toward better grades.

Opportunities for study vary so widely from person to person that specific recommendations about time and place are valueless. Those with jobs, those responsible for household duties, others who live long distances from school, and those involved in extracurricular activities, especially dramatics and athletics, have commitments that limit and restrict study conditions.

Some persons have quiet rooms of their own. Some have no place for study other than a living room or kitchen crowded with other people. Some must do the bulk of their studying in a library, study hall, or other semipublic place. Some have little opportunity for study other than on buses or trains or in automobiles. In many schools, students are required to be in study halls at specified times.

No matter what your circumstances, you should try to find out what conditions are best for you and seek to arrange for them to the limits of possibility. The somewhat general remarks that follow may not apply directly to you, but possibly you can alter, adapt, or adjust your study situations to them.

Where to Study

1. *Wherever you study, try to avoid distractions.*

Probably the best place for you to study is a room of your own with a door you can lock. If you are this fortunate, you may think that you are free from outside interferences. You are, but only if you force yourself to be. You will need to set up rules concerning yourself and others in the same house or building: no trips to answer the telephone, no response to visitors who knock on your door, no working on a favorite hobby, no gazing at admired photos, no playing of records or tapes. When you do take a needed and recommended short break, leave your desk or room entirely. Reserve them for study and nothing else during work periods. Following these suggestions will be difficult at first, but practice and resulting habit will make them easier as time passes.

Perhaps the most popular self-distraction is the radio, followed by television, records, and tapes. Large numbers of people insist that they can study better while listening to music or even watching television. They claim, for instance, that music helps them to concentrate on work at hand. No scientific tests have been made, but it is at least possible that music helps studying about as much as alcohol does driving an automobile. Both music and alcohol are "relaxers" for most people, but is relaxation what is most needed when one is driving a car or studying intently? You will not easily give up your radio, record player, and television set if using them has become an ingrained habit. But try an experiment: study for a week without them. You may uncover some startling differences in how much you can absorb and play back in your mind without background effects you previously considered essential.

2. *Discover where you study best and work there whenever possible.*

If you have a room to yourself and prefer it for study, use it as much as you can. If you derive comfort and strength from others who are also studying, then seek the companionship provided by a library or study hall. If you prefer such a semipublic place for studying but find that minor distractions disturb your concentration, retreat to your room, home, or some other place.

If you are accustomed to studying on a bus or train, are you bothered by movement and noise? If you are, close your eyes and rest or think. When you do arrive at your preferred study place, you may be refreshed, not tense, weary, or upset.

"You are you and I am I." That I choose one place for study and you prefer another is unimportant. Pick your optimum place for optimum study without regard for what hundreds of your fellow students seem to prefer. Whatever place is best for you *is* best for you, no matter what or where it is and no matter what anyone else thinks about it. But don't study at "any old place"; study at the spot where you feel you can be most receptive and most productive.

3. *Study is not a horizontal activity.*

A bed is for rest and sleep, among other things, not for study. A study chair is for sitting erect in, not reclining on the small of the back. Slouching in an easy chair is great for resting, snoozing, or reading a magazine, but slouching is not an ideal position for genuine study. Sitting erect in a comfortable chair is more conducive to real study in your own room, the library, or a study hall than any reclining or horizontal position known to man. Study is serious business that requires and deserves alertness of body as well as of mind.

4. *Organize your favorite study place.*

You may not have a room of your own for study. And yet nearly everyone can secure a carrel in a library, a desk in a study hall, or one corner of a room in the place where he or she lives. Assume that you have such a spot.

First, clear your desk of its clutter. Get rid of everything that does not relate to work in hand. The ideal desk arrangement is the simplest and barest possible. Books on your desk or on a shelf readily at hand should be those—and only those—that are actively to be used.

Second, having cleared your desk, make sure that your lighting—natural or artificial—is adequate and efficient. Shift your chair or desk. Get a better light bulb; move the light. Whatever is necessary, do it.

Third, examine your chair. If it does not allow you to sit comfortably erect, try another; adjust the height of the chair or the desk, or move to another location. Do whatever is needed to organize your body as well as your work space.

Fourth, make certain that you have at hand all the tools you will need, and do this *before* you begin studying. These tools include pens or pencils, textbooks, notebooks, erasers, writing paper, reference books, typewriter, or whatever. Failure to stock and organize your work space will cause lost time, loss of concentration, and unnecessary interruptions. But remember the guiding rule in study-space organization: everything needed but nothing superfluous. It's easy to overdo, to spend more time and effort in getting ready than in getting down to work. Speaking of his own writing room, that master stylist, E. B. White, once remarked that there is a subtle danger in life's refinements, that "one thing leads to another," and that "the first thing you know, the writer has a stuffed chair and is fast asleep in it."

When to Study

You may think differently, but not even the most zealous of your teachers expects you to study all the time. Neither should anyone else. Everyone understands the need for rest and relaxation. A laborer grows weary after hours of digging ditches. So does a conscientious student, because concentrated study is as tiring as digging ditches or any other activity man engages in. You are not expected to study *every* possible moment, but you need to put in long hours of regular study. What "long hours"?

If you know as much about yourself as you should, you recognize that you feel better, physically and mentally, at certain hours than at others. Our states of mind and body result from activities we have been engaging in and events that have occurred in our lives. Regardless of activities and events, however, we feel more physically alive and mentally alert at certain times of the day or week or month. What, for you, are these times? And when do you feel most sluggish and dull?

Supply your own answers to these two questions, but make your answers honest. Then try to do your hardest studying at your "best" times. This is an individual concern, but three general considerations apply to everyone:

1. *There are "day people" and "night people."*

Researchers differ somewhat in their findings about metabolism, sleep, and other processes by which energy is created. But you know from experience whether you greet a new day with relish and enthusiasm or feel dull and sluggish until noon or later. Some people claim they do their best work during morning hours. They may be right, for several physical and emotional reasons, including the one that they think so. Others "come alive" later in the day and accomplish as much in afternoon and evening hours as others do in a "normal" work day. They, too, may be correct, in part for the same reason.

Carefully examine your own states of mind and physical well-being. If possible, study during the hours you feel most alert and alive. At times when you feel you cannot apply yourself to hard study, perform the routine tasks that face all of us. If you find that you *never* feel physically and emotionally equipped to study, you'd better seek professional help or drop out of school. In everyone's day occur "dull" hours; in everyone's month are "lost" days. Realizing this truth should help you seize on the times that you feel productive and avoid the cop out of insisting that you never feel like studying or that you get poor results from the time you do put in. A change in schedule based on your energy and interest output will make a difference. Try it for yourself.

2. *Study in sizable time periods.*

Your daily schedule may prevent setting aside more than bits and pieces of time for study. That is unfortunate, because nearly all effective study requires a warm-up period followed by a fairly substantial block of time. Thirty minutes is usually not long enough to work into a subject and get a firm hold on it. Conversely, it is unwise to force yourself to study long hours without a break. Depending on the schedule you have, in and out of school, arrange for study periods of from one to three hours that will be broken only by brief rest minutes. If this plan won't work for you, then you should (1) rearrange your outside commitments or (2) rearrange your class schedule or (3) be satisfied with low grades. A fourth alternative, dropping out of school until you do have proper time for study, is not recommended but may be sensible.

3. *Be a full-time student.*

In some occupations you might be expected to put in a seven- or eight-hour day and no more. In others, work is never completed. In still others, workers do not do their jobs for even the minimum number of hours expected and required.

How about you? As a student, your job is to study and learn. Do you really work at it for as long hours as you would at some job outside school? Perhaps you do, but if so, you outdo the majority of students in school and college. Be honest. How many hours a day do you really devote to attentive classroom and laboratory work and genuine home and library study? All right—con yourself if you must.

But even if you do put in full hours of concentrated work, that is not enough. As someone developing mental powers and acquiring knowledge and skills, your tasks never really cease. You are (or should be) like a businessperson who leaves the office every night with a loaded briefcase or a homemaker who works at something every waking hour or a professional who thinks about legal or medical or other cases every hour he or she is conscious. A famous trial lawyer whose success was attributed by some to his luck remarked that his "luck" usually came to him in his study at 3:00 A.M. the day of a trial.

Do these remarks seem unreasonable? Remember that study is hard work and, furthermore, is the most rewarding and important work you will ever do—learning.

Yes, study is best accomplished in blocks of time, but scraps can be important, too. You can run over in your mind some topic or subject related to schoolwork while you are taking a bath, dressing, eating, or working at your regular job. Riding to school provides an opportunity for thinking about and reviewing what you studied the night before. Conversation in the cafeteria can occasionally be turned to some phase of classroom activity.

Everyone—yes, everyone—has brief moments every day that can be used, misused, or wasted. Profitably using some of these snippets of time is a practical, time-tested step toward getting greater satisfaction from your work and increased rewards for it.

Time is everyone's most precious and most squandered possession. You have more time for study than you realize, no matter how busy you are or think you are. Use it.

5

Work within a Time Budget

You may not be the smartest person in your class. You may not read as well or as fast as others do. You may not write and speak as clearly and effectively as your fellow students. But one thing you possess as fully as the brightest A student in any class: *time*.

How well or poorly we use time is important in every part of our lives, nowhere more so than in studying. You will have noted that some member of your family, or some friend or acquaintance, never seems frantic, never rushed. Such a person is always prepared ahead of time. He or she seems to accomplish more than others do. Perhaps you have envied such success and wondered how it is achieved. Perhaps you have often said to yourself, "Oh, I could do as well if only I had time."

Well, stop kidding yourself. Each of us has as much time as anyone else. It's true that some students have nothing to do but study—no household or family duties, no outside jobs, no long travel time to and from school, no sports, no extracurricular activities. Such demands on time are often heavy, but they are rarely as heavy as we like to think. Everyone—no exceptions—has time to do whatever he wants to do, provided he wants to do it badly enough.

Why is it that the busiest people in your school or community are invariably the first to be thought of when some new responsibility or task arises? Why are the most active persons assigned additional positions or chores? Why are some of your classmates unfailingly prepared for class recitation, never late with assigned papers, and never frightened into frantic tailspins before tests and examinations?

The answer is that such persons *value* and *organize* their time. They realize that time is everyone's most valuable possession, that it is, as Benjamin Franklin wrote in *Poor Richard's Almanac*, "the stuff life is made of." They understand, as Franklin also remarked, that "lost time is never found again." They might not know this stanza from "The Rubáiyát of Omar Khayyám," but they would agree that its message applies as much to time as it does to events:

> The moving finger writes, and, having writ,
> Moves on; nor all your Piety nor Wit
> Shall lure it back to cancel half a line,
> Nor all your Tears wash out a Word of it.

Yes, each of us wastes time. No, we don't really value it as we should. But it can hardly have escaped our notice that time has an economic value. If you hold an outside job, you are most likely paid on a time basis: by the hour, day, week, or month. Plumbers, electricians, carpenters, auto mechanics, and all other maintenance and repairmen charge "by the hour." Lawyers, accountants, and other professionals keep records of time spent and render bills accordingly. If you are foolish enough to protest a physician's bill for services rendered in five minutes, you will get some response concerning the months and years the doctor spent preparing to render that service.

Everyone's time has value, but it attains its true worth only when it is organized intelligently and used sensibly. A homemaker plans a day and allots a certain time for this task, another stretch of time for that. Most businesspeople plot their activities in advance, sometimes weeks and months ahead. No effectively producing member of society consistently goes through life "taking things as they come." Periodically, interruptions occur, but the main idea is to get back on the time track as soon as possible.

In most learning situations, much of your time is planned for you. You are allotted certain hours in classroom or laboratory. But what about the minutes and hours that are not laid out for you? The total of such periods is probably greater than you think. Do you organize and use them in any way resembling their worth? If you don't, all other practices suggested in this book will lose much of their potential effectiveness.

Learning to use time is a valuable acquired skill, one that will pay dividends not only in studying but all through life. In fact, the ability to use time efficiently may well be one of the most significant achievements of your entire life.

This chapter can realistically hope to accomplish only two things. The first is to get you to do some thinking about the value of time, *your* time. If you weren't taking a class or classes, what would you be doing on the outside and how much would you be paid for doing it? Have you ever compared the lifetime earnings of the "average" high school graduate with those of persons who did not get that far in their schooling? With the earnings of a college graduate? On an entirely practical basis, the hours spent in furthering your education may have potential value far exceeding what you could expect to be paid for outside work.

Aside from monetary values, time spent in study can increase your worth to society as an understanding, thoughtful, aware, compassionate, and responsible human being. But values such as these will not be obvious to you if you so misuse time as to feel that study is unrewarding, neither pleasurable nor exciting. If you are bored, restless, and impatient to get into what you call "the real world," you neither value school time correctly nor use it properly.

The second aim of this chapter is to cause you to think about the wisdom, the common sense, of organizing—of budgeting—your time. You know what a budget is: an estimate, often itemized, of income and expense. Well, your "income" is twenty-four hours a day. Your "expense" is the spending, the using, of time each day. A budget is a plan of operation. A time budget is an allotment of amounts of time to be spent in specified periods. As you well know, "time is money."

Neither this book nor any other can accurately tell you precisely how to budget your time. You may be engaged in full-time work. You may have a job after school hours or on weekends. Certain courses require more time than others, not necessarily the same courses for all students. If you are an efficient reader, you may need to spend only half as much time on English or history as on a science or math course. If you are a slow and inefficient reader, the reverse could be true. You may have a "light" or "heavy" schedule of classes. Considerations such as these make all "canned" schedules worthless.

The best procedure is to plan your own study schedule to fit your circumstances and those of no one else. This you *can* do. This you *should* do if you wish to get value received from schoolwork. This you *must* do if you wish to reduce worry, anxiety, and frustration and simultaneously raise your grades.

Adapt and apply these five suggestions to your own time schedule:

1. *Look ahead.*

If you have an option, don't overload your course schedule. If you are a slow reader, avoid taking more than one course at a time that requires heavy reading. Only rare students can simultaneously take two science courses with laboratory sessions. If you know that some particular course, such as English composition or U.S. history or algebra, is going to be difficult for you, try to schedule it in a semester with "easier" courses. If some team you are on requires long practice hours, try to take your toughest courses at some other time. In a given semester, try to balance courses in which you can do relatively well with one or more that you expect to be difficult.

Guidance counselors, course advisers, and previous teachers can help you. Also, talk to students who have taken courses ahead of you. Their advice can be helpful. In short, use your head and the heads of others. Some shifting and juggling is usually possible even with required courses. Plan ahead.

2. *Find out what each course demands.*

As early as you can, ascertain the kind and amount of work a course will require during a term or year. Many teachers do not give daily assignments, but nearly all will inform you early, orally or in a mimeographed syllabus, just what will be expected in outside reading, laboratory work, library study, papers, and the like. Until you have a fairly clear idea of what will be expected, you cannot plan a sensible time budget. If this information is hard to come by, ask other students who have taken the course. Better still, consult the teacher. All good teachers prefer to have their students know in advance what will be expected and precisely how those requirements will be rewarded or penalized in course grades.

3. *Prepare a tentative study plan.*

With courses set and general requirements understood, you can now allocate what study time you have. In doing this, you must be your own guide. Ideally, you will have a considerable block of time (one to three hours) each day for preparation of the next day's work. This allotment will vary in length from day to day—depending upon the subjects involved, assignments in them, outside commitments, and your aptitudes for particular courses. Classes on one day may require more preparation time than others. When this occurs (and it frequently does) use the free time on easy study afternoons or nights to work on assignments for tough days.

It is unwise, perhaps even stupid, to study an hour one day and five hours the next. Your study plan should be based on a week of work. When research projects or other intricate and lengthy outside assignments are involved, your study plan should stretch over several weeks or even months.

4. *Alter your study plan from time to time.*

In most courses, you will need several days or weeks to find out how much is required and how much study time to apportion. You can alter your tentative study plan as requirements become clearer, as outside assignments are made, and as work in other courses increases or decreases. A study plan should be your guide, not your master. Of course it should be altered when extracurricular activities such as sports and social events occur, but never forget or neglect a study plan and as quickly as possible return to it in its original or modified form.

5. *Actively use your study plan.*

The best possible study plan is worthless unless you follow it conscientiously and consistently. It's only too easy to borrow time from your plan and never repay it. Results will be erratic and uneven if you follow a plan for two or three weeks and then start to slight it. If your plan calls for an hour of study for Course A on Wednesdays, then put in that hour every Wednesday or unfailingly make it up. Regular, organized, planned study is a concrete step toward better performance and better grades.

The preceding paragraphs have dealt with planned study time, solid chunks of one, two, three or more hours. But what about the snippets of time at your disposal? How do you spend the few minutes you have between classes? What about the twenty or thirty minutes left during the lunch hour? What do you do in a free period?

Perhaps these five- or fifty-minute breaks seem too brief to be useful. Possibly they can best be used for relaxing and talking with friends. Perhaps. But never forget that these periods add up. They are frequently wasted. And they represent time, valuable time. Give some thought to making occasional, frequent, or regular use of these segments of time.

Many writers have commented that they write all the time, not merely when they're putting words on paper. They write in their heads, or, as one author has put it, "on the hoof" as they gc about daily tasks—walking, talking, riding, eating, taking a bath, dressing, reading, and even sleeping. An "absent-minded" professor may be "present-minded" because he or she is thinking actively about a subject but not about where he is walking or what he seems to be doing. Many a scientist is working when he is nowhere near laboratory or books.

You are not a professional writer, professor, or scientist, but as a student you can profitably use fragments of otherwise wasted time for reviewing class work and thinking about forthcoming assignments.

Actually, you can do substantial reading and studying in brief segments of time, provided you really want to. Let's assume that you are an "average" reader, capable of reading 300 words a minute of material of medium difficulty. In fifteen minutes you can read 4500 words. This means that in fifteen minutes a day you can read 31,500 words in a week and some 130,000 words in a month. This last figure is the length of a full-sized book. Kept up for a year, fifteen-minute daily reading periods would enable you to cover a dozen or more books.

Is this really possible? The answer is yes, and proof is available from any persons who have done just this. Of course you need the will to use this time and you must make sure that you always have reading material available. But it's not difficult to slip a book into your clothing or pocketbook when you are dressing. You can keep a book at your bedside. You can place one in the bathroom.

All of us waste time, but some of us waste more than others. Look around you in classrooms, in halls, in the cafeteria, library, and dormitory. You get the picture, don't you? Using time properly will let you be a part of the solution, not the problem.

Budgeting time is valuable for everyone from preadolescence through old age, in school and out. Consider this comment by a prominent college official:

> The greatest single shortcoming of incoming students is their inability to use the large amounts of unscheduled time on their hands. And the greatest cause of dropouts and failures is not stupidity, lack of preparation, or even a sort of vague unwillingness to work and learn. It's wasting and misusing time inside and outside of classrooms and laboratories.

Sensible budgeting of time, however limited that time may seem or really be, underlies every activity and tool suggested in this book. It also underlies every activity you will engage in as long as you live.

6

Try to Think Logically and Clearly

Education has been defined in many ways, but a consensus is that it is the process of acquiring general knowledge and developing powers of reasoning and judgment. These two aims are closely related; the first is wholly dependent upon the second. Thinking—or what we call thinking—directly causes and shapes our every act, emotional response, and point of view.

But, as has often been remarked, we rarely think about thinking and are constantly confused by the odd and faulty ideas we have about it. Much of what we call thinking is ingrained habit, controlled response, rationalization, and daydreaming. The British playwright George Bernard Shaw once suggested that we use our reason only to support our prejudices.

Perhaps we rarely think about thinking because thinking is hard to do. Possibly we believe we get along fairly well without doing much of it. Probably we think we're thinking when actually we are doing nothing of the sort. "If you make people think they're thinking," Don Marquis, an American humorist, once wrote, "they'll love you. If you make them think, they'll hate you."

It's possible to graduate from school or college without ever doing any genuine thinking. Presumably, millions of people have done just this. And yet it seems certain that the experience of school would have been far more meaningful if they had tried to learn something about thinking and had occasionally done some. It's equally certain that had they done so, their grades would have been remarkably better.

Errors in thinking and reasoning can destroy fact-finding papers. They can defeat classroom responses as well as talks that try to establish a case or prove a point. They can ruin grades in mathematics, physics, chemistry, history, philosophy, and indeed in almost any course.

Being human, each of us readily and consistently ignores, twists, or exaggerates evidence and established facts. Being human, we think what we want to think. We protect our prejudices and fixed beliefs. We resent opposing ideas. Being human, we often scorn logic and flout common sense. Being human, we lessen our chances for getting higher grades by not thinking at all, by careless thinking, and by faulty and illogical thinking.

You may consider yourself a rational person and believe that every statement you make and every sentence you write is reasonable. If so, think again. Neither you nor I nor anyone else can make every statement reasonable because reasoning is based upon facts or what are considered facts. And facts, or assumed facts, change with time. For example, the facts of medicine or physics or population growth or air pollution only a few years ago are hardly the *facts* today. Reasoning is also based upon conclusions drawn from facts; yet the conclusions one reasonable individual draws from a given set of facts may differ widely from those of another person.

Clearly, then, you cannot make your every statement reasonable. But at least you can avoid making statements that are obviously questionable; and if you do make such a statement, you should be prepared to defend it. You should make your meaning clear by offering evidence. You can usually avoid statements based on faulty premises, those based on false analogy, those involving mere generalizations. How logical, for example, are these statements?

> All motor vehicles should have governors limiting their speed to 55 miles an hour. (What about police cars? ambulances? fire trucks?)
>
> Since football is the most dangerous of all sports, my parents refused to allow me to play it. (Overlook the possible parental muddleheadedness: What about water polo? bullfighting? skin-diving?)
>
> Steve knows all there is to know about stocks and bonds. (All? Absolutely nothing he doesn't know?)
>
> Gambling is a bad habit; everyone should avoid it because habits are bad. (Can you prove gambling is a bad habit? Are habits bad? All habits? What about the habit of paying your debts? Telling the truth?)

You may also believe that you possess a logical mind. Indeed, if you accept a definition of logic as "logical reasoning," you may be partially right. If you agree with this quotation from *Alice's Adventures in Wonderland*, you certainly are right: "Contrariwise," continued Tweedledee, "if it was so, it might be; and if it were so, it would be; but if it isn't, it ain't. That's logic."

Induction and Deduction

It is likely that you, like all other people, use and abuse two common methods of thinking every day. These methods are *induction* and *deduction.*

The former seeks to establish a general truth, an all-embracing principle or conclusion. The inductive process begins by using observation of specific facts, which it classifies. From a sufficient number of these facts, or particulars, the inductive process leads into a general principle, a comprehensive conclusion. Movement of thought is from the *particular* to the *general.*

Deduction, conversely, tries to show how a particular statement is true because it is part of, and leads down from, a general principle or truth. Movement of thought is from the *general* to the *particular.*

In *inductive* reasoning a set of particulars is studied experimentally and, from observations made, a general principle is drawn or formed. For example: Every horse I have seen has four legs; therefore, I can expect all horses to have four legs. In *deductive* reasoning an accepted general statement, which may be true or false, is applied to a particular situation or case. For example: All horses are animals; this is a horse; therefore, this is an animal.

Processes of thought such as these may seem different from your own thinking processes. Nevertheless, all people do reason this way. For example, early in history, men became convinced that no one lives forever, that sooner or later all men die. Through inductive thinking, mankind arrived at a general conclusion: All men are mortal.

A generalization as well established as this, one that needs neither reexamination nor further testing, may be used as a starting point, that is, a *premise* in deductive thinking. In light of the general truth that all men are mortal, we examine the future of a man named Ned Weston. This deductive process may be expressed in the form of a *syllogism*:

Major premise:	All men are mortal.
Minor premise:	Ned Weston is a man.
Conclusion:	Ned Weston is mortal.

Although we do not arrange our thoughts in syllogisms such as the one just illustrated, we reason in much the same way. For example, we assume that events encountered in the future will be like those met with in the past. What, indeed, is the real meaning of the saying "A burnt child dreads the fire"?

In induction, the possibility of exceptions always exists, but those general conclusions reached by inductive processes are usually acceptable. When you write "Most honor graduates of high school do well in college," you cannot be certain because you cannot have examined all records of past and present students and cannot be positive about the future. But the statement is probable. So is the inductive conclusion that no two people have identical fingerprints or footprints, although this statement, too, is only theoretically capable of being positively proved.

Through inductive reasoning, the laws (the principles, the generalized and descriptive statements) of any science, such as chemistry and physics, have been arrived at. Through deductive reasoning they are applied in particular situations: the launching of a space rocket, the manufacture of a computer, the development of a vaccine. In pure and applied science, such reasoning is virtually foolproof. But loopholes do occur where human beings and human behavior are concerned.

Logical Loopholes

Here is brief observation on nine of the more common offenses against straight and logical thinking:

1. *Hasty generalization*

The most prevalent error in inductive reasoning is observing only a few instances and then jumping to an invalid conclusion. For instance, you know a few athletes you consider stupid; does it follow that all, or even most, athletes are mentally deficient? What is the specific evidence for labeling certain groups "hippie freaks," "irresponsible woman drivers," "dumb blondes," "male chauvinist pigs"? What is the evidence for "every schoolboy knows . . ." or "all good Americans realize . . ." or "statistics show . . ."?

2. *Non sequitur*

A major error in deductive thinking is the "it does not follow" assumption. *Non sequitur* is an inference or conclusion that does not proceed from the premises or materials upon which it is apparently based. This fallacy can be caused by a false major premise and by a minor premise that is only apparently related to the major premise. For example, some good professional writers admit to being poor spellers. Are you justified in concluding that you, too, also a poor speller, are destined to be a good professional writer? These syllogisms illustrate the *non sequitur* flaw in thinking:

> All members of X club are conceited.
> Frances is not a member of X club.
> Therefore, Frances is not conceited.
>
> Some members of X club are conceited.
> Frances is a member of X club.
> Therefore, Frances is conceited.

3. *Post hoc, ergo propter hoc*

A name applied to a variation of hasty generalization, *post hoc, ergo propter hoc* means in English "after this, therefore on account of this." The error it involves is to hold that a happening which precedes another must naturally or necessarily be its cause or that when one event follows another the latter event is the result of the first. "I have a cold today because I got my feet wet yesterday." "No wonder I had bad luck today; I walked under a ladder yesterday." The Roman Empire fell after the birth and spread of Christianity. Would anyone argue that Christianity alone directly caused the fall of Rome? Those who do (and many have) make the *post hoc, ergo propter hoc* mistake in reasoning.

4. *Biased or suppressed evidence*

Facts that furnish ground for belief and help to prove an assumption or proposition constitute evidence. An obvious flaw in reasoning is selecting evidence from questionable sources or omitting evidence that runs contrary to the point you wish to make. The testimony of dedicated yoga disciples is in itself not sufficient to prove that practicing yoga promotes a peaceful mind or a healthful, happy life. What do those who do not practice yoga think? What do physicians and philosophers think? other authorities? recent converts? those who once practiced yoga and have given it up?

Figures and statistics can lie if evidence is biased or suppressed. Many of the so-called truths we hear and read have been prepared by paid propagandists and directly interested individuals or groups. Biased and suppressed evidence has caused everyone to recognize that "figures don't lie, but liars figure."

5. *Distinguishing fact from opinion*

A fact is based on actuality of some sort, a *verifiable* event or statement, whereas opinion is an inference that may be mingled with a supposed fact. That Ernest Hemingway was "an American writer" is a statement which can be proved. That Hemingway was "the greatest American novelist of the twentieth century" is only an opinion of those who hold it. That Thomas Jefferson was President from 1801 until the inauguration of James Madison in 1809 is a fact; that Jefferson was "our greatest President" is a matter of opinion. A favorite device of many writers and speakers is to mingle opinions with facts and thus obscure the difference between them.

6. *Begging the question*

This flaw in thinking consists of taking a conclusion for granted before it is proved or assuming in the propositions (premises) that which is to be proved in the conclusion. A question such as "Should a vicious man like Charles Grundy be allowed to hold office?" is loaded because it assumes what needs to be proved. Common forms of begging the question are *slanting, name-calling,* and *shifting the meaning of the word.*

Using unfairly suggestive words to create an emotional attitude (as in the application of *vicious* to Charles Grundy, above) is a form of slanting. It is also a form of *argumentum ad hominem,* a Latin phrase meaning "argument against the person"—an argument against the person who may hold an opinion rather than against the opinion itself: "Only an idiot would believe that."

Guard against using or fully believing such suggestive words and phrases as *bigoted, saintly, progressive, reactionary, undemocratic ideas,* or *dangerous proposal.* Use them if you have supporting evidence; accept them if the proof offered seems valid. Otherwise, avoid slanting in writing and be on your guard when reading and listening.

Name-calling is closely allied to slanting. It appeals to prejudice and emotion rather than to intellect. It employs "good" words to approve and accept, "bad" words to condemn and reject. In writing and talking, be cautious in using such terms as *two-faced, yes man, angel in disguise, rabblerouser, benefactor, do-gooder,* and so on.

Shifting the meaning of a word consists of using the same word several times with a shift in meaning designed to confuse the reader or listener. A *conservative* disposed to preserve existing conditions and to agree with gradual rather than abrupt changes is one thing; a *conservative* unswervingly opposed to all progress, a reactionary, is another. Student *unions* are one thing; labor *unions* are another. Should every citizen vote the Republican ticket because ours is a great *republic* or vote the *Democratic* ticket because this is a great *democracy*?

7. *Evading the issue*

This error in logic is most common in heated arguments. It consists of ignoring the point under discussion and making a statement that has no bearing on the argument. If you tell a friend that he drives too fast and he responds that you are a poor driver yourself, he has evaded the issue. He may be right, but he has neither met your objection nor won the argument. Such argument is especially common in political campaigns. It is easy to sidestep an issue and launch a counterattack.

8. *Faulty analogy*

Because two objects or ideas are alike in one or more respects, they are not necessarily similar in some further way. *Analogy* (partial similarity) can be both accurate and effective; otherwise we could not employ either similes or metaphors. But when we use figurative-language analogy, we do not expect such a figure of speech to *prove* anything.

In the kind of writing most of us do most of the time, an analogy is chiefly useful as an illustration. In many analogies, differences outweigh similarities. "Why do we need Social Security? Do we help trees when they lose their leaves in autumn winds? Do we provide assistance to dogs and horses in their old age? Don't some tribes kill people when they are too old to be useful?" Such analogy as this is obviously absurd, but even more literal analogies than this can be ridiculous. You may, for example, reason that since the honor system has worked well in several small colleges, it will work equally well in large universities. Are the similarities between the schools either superficial or less important than the differences? The whipping post was a deterrent to crime in seventeenth-century New England. Is it false analogy to suggest that similar punishment should be inflicted on twentieth-century criminals and dope addicts?

9. *Testimonials*

Citing statements from historical personages or well-known contemporaries is not necessarily straight thinking. In an attempt to bolster an argument, we are quick to employ such terms as *authorities have concluded, science proves, doctors say, laboratory tests reveal*. George Washington, Thomas Jefferson, and Abraham Lincoln—justly renowned as they are—might not have held economic, social, and political views necessarily valid in the twentieth century. Douglas MacArthur was a great military strategist, but something he said about combustion engines may be less convincing than the words of a good local mechanic. Is an authority in one field an oracle of wisdom about any subject on which he speaks or writes? As a witness for or against an important educational policy, how effective would an eminent surgeon be? a football hero? a TV personality? If you were writing an attack on vaccination, would you reasonably expect the opposition of George Bernard Shaw to outweigh the pronouncements of the entire medical profession?

But even where there is little question of the validity of authority, be careful that neither bias nor the time element weakens your presentation. Some business executives and labor leaders are experts on economic problems, but their particular interests might prevent their having the impartiality, the objectivity, of a disinterested observer. As for timing, remember that in many fields of human activity and knowledge, authorities soon become obsolete. Charles Darwin no longer has the last word on evolution; Sigmund Freud is not universally considered the final authority in psychoanalysis.

Checklist for Written Work

Before submitting a paper, apply the following comments to forestall their being made by someone else. (For the suggestions in this checklist the author is indebted to Professor Macklin Thomas, formerly of the Department of Higher Education, Chicago.)

1. The statement needs qualification; it is too sweeping or dogmatic. (This comment refers to assertions that are not altogether false or irresponsible but simply cover too much ground too positively and need to be guarded with a limiting phrase or clause specifying the degree of certainty warranted, taking account of possible exceptions, or confining the generalization to what you are reasonably sure of.)
2. The facts cited are not such as are likely to be accepted on your bare assertion. You should supply informally in the current of your development some authority, occupational experience, or other reason why you should be believed.
3. Your argument is good so far as it goes, but it is unconvincing because you have failed to dispose of some obvious and overriding argument that can be made on the other side. Your case is strengthened when you evaluate your own argument and show that you have disposed of possible alternatives.
4. The evidence supplied is pertinent but falls far short of proof. One good reason does not build a case.
5. There is such a thing as being too specific if you do not make clear what generalization is supported by the instances given. A well-developed train of thought works back and forth between the general and the specific, showing the connections and applications intended at each point.

6. Your treatment here is obviously marked by particular bias and prior emotional commitment. This does not necessarily make your conclusions false, but it does make them all suspect.

7. Your approach here is essentially moralistic and directive rather than analytical. No law exists against preaching, but distinguish preaching from investigation, analysis, and reasoning.

8. Here you are exploring religious or philosophical questions that have been discussed for thousands of years without being resolved. You of course have a right to try your hand at them, but don't expect an easy success, and remember that no certain conclusions are possible when the assumptions with which you start out are untestable.

In itself, learning about the kinds of illogical or crooked thinking everyone engages in will not materially improve anyone's thought processes. But becoming aware that many statements we make, in and out of class, can probably be challenged on some ground should alert us to the need for straight thinking. Some answers to questions are obviously incorrect. Others may be partly right and partly wrong, with the "wrong" part caused by fuzzy thinking of some sort.

Straightening out crooked thinking is difficult. It may even seem a vague and inconclusive step toward better grades. But it will appear neither hazy nor indefinite to most of your teachers.

7

Understand What You Read

If asked to give one reason for the low grades you may be getting, would you make any of these statements?

1. I hate studying and therefore do as little as possible.
2. All my courses are dull and boring.
3. I've so much to do that I've little time for studying.
4. Teachers don't really want to help me.
5. If I knew how to study I'd do more of it.
6. The important things I want to know are not taught in any school.
7. I get low grades only in courses I don't like.
8. My mind jumps about too much.
9. Poor marks discourage me so much that I get turned off.
10. I've never learned to read as well as I should.

Each of these statements makes sense of a sort. Each has been offered by many students. You may select any one of them or may decide that several apply equally well. You may give still another reason. These ten responses, however, were made most often in multiple-choice tests given to randomly selected groups of 210 high school and college students.

Regardless of your choice, a good case can be made for Number 10. In fact, numerous teachers and experts in "how to study" methods agree that it outweighs other causes of poor work. They insist that most of the other nine reasons are caused by Number 10. They feel strongly that inability to read up to one's potential is a prime contributor to boredom, restlessness, lack of desire to do well, and over-all discouragement.

You may not agree. "How," you say, "can this be so? I learned to read in the first grade and have been reading ever since. Of course I can read. How would I have got this far if I couldn't?"

You have a point. You can read. But how well can you read? Can you read rapidly enough to keep up with assignments? Do you constantly find difficult the vocabulary of what you're reading? Do you have to go back again and again to reread an assignment? Is it hard for you to put into your own words summaries of what you read?

Honest answers to these questions should convince anyone—no exceptions—that he or she does not read as well as he would like to and probably needs to. No one is a perfect reader; everyone has reading deficiencies. We should, however, face the solid fact that no skill acquired in school years can be more helpful and valuable, now and in later life, than the abilities to (1) understand what we read and (2) read with reasonable speed. Steady, determined improvement in these abilities is a sure step toward better grades, inner satisfactions, and changed attitudes toward the entire process of living and learning.

Thomas Carlyle, a Scottish historian and essayist, put the matter clearly: "If we think of it, all that a university can do for us is but what the first school began doing—teach us to read."

Learning to read efficiently is a long and difficult task. Perhaps it should be both time-consuming and occasionally arduous, because reading is miraculous when we stop to think that through it we have at our command and for our daily use much of the best that has been thought and written by the greatest minds of many centuries.

But remarks here should not be considered as overly stressing the dullness and difficulty of reading at the expense of the pleasure and excitement it affords many millions of readers. After all, reading is one of the few pure pleasures (some say the only one) known to humankind. Reading can be a delight, a pastime that, in the words of the great English writer Sir Philip Sidney, "holdeth children from play and old men from the chimney corner."

Although you may not be among their number, many persons actually read for enjoyment and sheer pleasure "heavy" works dealing with science, biography, history, and the like. One's active sympathies and intellectual curiosity strongly affect what and how one reads.

Reading for Comprehension

Much of our reading is neither accurate nor thoughtful. When we read a newspaper, a light short story, a mystery, or a comic book, we are seeking relaxation and naturally skip and skim. Ordinarily such reading fare as this neither deserves nor receives careful attention and subsequent reviewing. But often we attempt similarly to read meaty fiction and drama, closely reasoned essays, carefully wrought poems, and fact-packed textbooks. When we do, we receive little of the meaning intended and thus grow bored or discouraged. Reading to understand does not necessarily mean reading with speed and never involves reading with inattention and lack of concentration. The reading of genuinely important material must be painstakingly careful. In *Translating Literature into Life*, Arnold Bennett wrote:

> What is the matter with our reading is casualness, languor, preoccupation. We don't give the book a chance. We don't put ourselves at the disposal of the book. It is impossible to read properly without using all one's engine-power. If we are not tired after reading, common sense is not in us. How should one grapple with a superior mind and not be out of breath?
>
> But even if we read with the whole force of our brain, and do nothing else, common sense is still not in us, while sublime conceit is. For we are assuming that, without further trouble, we can possess, coordinate, and assimilate all the ideas and sensations rapidly offered to us by a mind greater than our own. The assumption has only to be stated in order to appear in its monstrous absurdity. Hence it follows that something remains to be done. This something is the act of reflection. Reading without subsequent reflection is ridiculous; it is equally a proof of folly and of vanity.

Bennett used the word *reflection* to mean "evaluation," analysis, thinking through and putting the author's words into one's own way of saying things (see Chapter 11).

In reading to understand, to comprehend, keep in mind that everyone ought to learn to read well enough to

1. Gain and understand accurate information and ideas.
2. Recognize the organization and style of what he is reading.
3. Interpret what he is reading in terms of his own experience.
4. Analyze, evaluate, and paraphrase what he is reading.

Whether we read for relaxation, information, or both, our aim should be to use our time intelligently. More than three centuries ago, Francis Bacon wrote as wisely as anyone ever has on the relationship of reading and writing:

> Read not to contradict and confute; nor to believe and take for granted; nor to find talk and discourse; but to weigh and consider. Some books are to be tasted, others to be swallowed, and some

few to be chewed and digested; that is, some books are to be read only in parts; others to be read, but not curiously; and some few to be read wholly, and with diligence and attention. Some books also may be read by deputy, and extracts made of them by others; but that would be only in the less important arguments, and the meaner sort of books; else distilled books are like common distilled waters, flashy things. Reading maketh a full man; conference a ready man; and writing an exact man. And therefore, if a man write little, he had need have a great memory; if he confer little, he had need have a present wit; and if he read little, he had need have much cunning, to seem to know what he doth not.

As you try to increase your reading ability, a process that should continue as long as you live, occasionally refer to these

TEN COMMANDMENTS FOR READING WITH COMPREHENSION

1. Determine and expect to remember what you read.
2. Remember that reading is *thinking with the author.*
3. Concentrate; read while you read and do nothing else.
4. Read at varying rates, slowing down or speeding up as the difficulty or ease of the material dictates.
5. Look up words whose meanings you don't know.
6. Investigate unfamiliar references and allusions.
7. Study accompanying diagrams, charts, graphs, and footnotes.
8. Look for main ideas; concentrate on chapter headings and topic sentences. (Reading is not primarily a matter of words and phrases. It is concerned with ideas. Look for them.)
9. As you read, make notes mentally or in your notebook.
10. Constantly practice summarizing (paraphrasing) each paragraph or main topic after you have read it. Do the same for a complete assignment.

Speed in Reading

Reading effectively is reading with both understanding and speed. By a conspiracy of silence, until recent years little attention was given to rapid reading. But the necessity for reading with reasonable rapidity has finally been recognized, and numerous steps have been taken to achieve this end. The necessity for learning to skip and scan certain kinds of material is now considered as important as learning to read other kinds of material with care and concentration.

An efficient reader reads thought units, not word-by-word. The technique involved is connected with the number of fixations the eyes make as they move across a page. Our aim should be to reduce the number of fixations, to lengthen the span of our eye movements. Our reading rate will increase as we learn to do this efficiently, and so will our comprehension. A skillful reader does not work with isolated units but with context—what precedes and follows the particular material he is looking at. A good reader rarely loses time by having to refer to the beginning of a sentence or paragraph he has finished. Rather he will have carried the thought through in one series of lengthened glances.

Here is another way to explain the process. The eye may be called the camera of the mind. It makes a snapshot; the brain then develops the film, prints the picture, and files away the results in what we call the mind. In reading, one's eyes must focus on what is being read before a picture can be taken; therefore the central purpose of rapid reading is to increase one's span of vision, reduce fixation time, and make more pictures.

The best advice in learning to read with speed as well as comprehension is "read with your head, not with your eyes." Doing this will enlarge comprehension by reducing the number of fixations and increase concentration. Practice finding main thoughts in a passage and separating them from subordinate thoughts; learn to find key words and key sentences and to distinguish them from purely illustrative material. These steps will greatly increase reading speed without reducing the even more important matter of comprehension.

Many institutions of learning maintain a special reading class or laboratory designed solely for the purpose of helping one learn to read with greater speed and understanding; if yours does, consult your teacher about it.

The reading rate of the general literate population of this country is about 250 words a minute with an attained comprehension of about 70 percent. This may seem a rapid rate, but actually it is about the sixth-grade level. You should be able to read more rapidly than this, although you must never forget that different kinds of material require different reading speeds.

In trying to learn to read more rapidly, consider these suggestions:

1. Time your reading speed. With a stopwatch or a watch with a second hand, find out how many words a minute you cover while reading (1) a newspaper, (2) a light magazine story, (3) one of your textbooks. You may find yourself reading 500 words a minute or more. You may discover that in order fully to understand a textbook in history or math or logic or physics, you need to spend an hour on a single page. What you find will be a guide in going about improving both understanding and speed.

2. Read a section (perhaps two or three pages) of one of your textbooks at a rapid rate, say 400 to 500 words a minute. After doing this, write a brief statement concerning its main ideas. Then read the same passage at 200 words a minute and look again at the statement you have written. Were you able to get the principal thought while reading rapidly? Did you miss a lot? Repeating this exercise several times with different material will enable you to find out how rapidly you can read and still comprehend with reasonable accuracy and fullness.

3. Give some thought to this question: Am I really such a

slow reader that I can't keep up or do I (1) fail to allow enough time for reading or (2) daydream instead of concentrating on what I'm doing? If it's a matter of time, not speed, see Chapter 5. If it's daydreaming, read Chapter 8 immediately or try another experiment: Time yourself on a passage to which you are giving complete attention and on a similar section without a deliberate effort to focus on the job. What you discover may indicate that you're more inattentive than you are slow.

This chapter has tried to make two main points: (1) Efficient reading is the single most useful tool you can acquire for the enjoyment of schoolwork, enrichment of life, and increased rewards in both grades and self-esteem. (2) Flexibility in reading speed is not just important, it's essential. Your skill as a reader is directly reflected in your ability to shift gears from one reading assignment to the next.

8

Get Rid of Bad Reading Habits

You may agree with everything in Chapter 7 but be handicapped in becoming a better reader by habits acquired in the past. If so, you have plenty of company. In reading, as in all other activities, everyone has formed harmful habits. The purpose of this chapter is to identify and comment on six faulty practices. If any apply to you, you can start to work on them. If none do, you are a miracle beyond compare.

First, all of us are deficient in *what* we have read. No matter how avidly you have read in the past, you have ignored or overlooked much that you feel you should have read. So have I. So has everyone. At present, we lack the necessary background to absorb fully everything we are now engaged in reading. Scientific and literary references, allusions, terms, and examples are often meaningless because of our comparative ignorance. Even the diction and style of some writers puzzle us. But as good or at least improving readers, we keep trying and continue to attack reading matter that often bewilders us.

Deficient and inadequate as we are, however, we are still

better off than people who have fallen into the bad habit of rarely reading anything. There are millions such. They will say, when questioned, that "reading is a waste of time," that "it's useless," that "living is what life is all about," that they "hate to read" or are "bored" by reading. The worst possible reading habit is not reading at all. The next worst is reading only one kind of simple material, such as newspapers, comic books, cartoons, or adventure or love stories.

The general situation seems to be this: Some people are good readers who have the capacity to become better ones. Some are virtual nonreaders who will be forced to improve their reading ability if they expect to get through whatever school they are attending. As a good, fair, or poor reader, you are probably letting one or all of the following habits prevent you from broadening your knowledge and expanding your horizons, thus making you ever more dependent upon TV and radio.

1. *Lack of concentration*

Sticking to the job at hand is never easy, whether you are learning a sport, doing housework, or engaging in any but the most exciting activities. Concentration is stressed at several places in this book precisely because all genuine mental activity is dependent upon close attention and stick-to-it-iveness. We know this but often seem to forget. But do you forget to concentrate when you are driving a car or riding a motorcycle? Probably not, because you realize that many accidents are caused by drivers who temporarily fail to focus on what they're doing. Many failures in reading are caused by the same neglect. It's time to learn and never forget that no matter what we are involved in, sooner or later our attention will flag, our interest will lag, and we'll start thinking about something other than what we are doing. The mind can be turned on and off like a light bulb. "Jumping the track" is all the easier and more natural when we are doing something that is difficult, demanding, and tiring. Reading properly is all of these.

How to lick this problem? Perhaps you can only partially overcome the difficulty, but here are three suggestions that may help:

First, make a conscious and deliberate effort of will to read with alert attention. Force yourself to focus on the page before you. Tell yourself that you *can* master the material in front of you. Keep reassuring yourself that you confidently expect to do just that. Giving yourself pep talks won't win the struggle, but it will help.

Second, every few minutes, stop reading for a few seconds or a couple of minutes. Close your eyes for a moment. Wash your face and hands in cool water. Stand up for ten seconds. But don't relax for so long that your mind wanders to other matters and you forget the job at hand. A momentary break should help you get back to the job at hand with renewed interest and attention.

Third, keep trying to focus hard on what you're reading and keep on trying day after day. Results may be poor at first. They probably will be. But as you read with greater concentration week after week, the task will become easier and more natural. Try it; you'll see.

2. *Regression*

As the word is used here, *regression* means going back over what you have been reading to pick up missed words or phrases or going back to find meanings lost because of daydreaming (thinking of something else) while you thought you were actually reading. Some of what we read *should* be gone over again, perhaps several times. But there's no good reason for regressing again and again to discover what we should have seen the first time. The reason many people can't keep up with reading is that they waste blocks of time not in reading or even rereading but in painfully going over the same material again and again. Every reader engages in some regression. The aim is to avoid *constant* regression.

3. *Lip reading*

As a child learning to read, you may have phrased words with your lips. You may never have outgrown the habit. Millions of readers haven't. If you move your lips when you read, you are a word reader—a person who simply cannot read with desirable speed and one who probably has difficulty with understanding as well. Find out if you are a lip reader. Don't say you aren't until you have proof. Hold a finger to your lips while reading. Or watch yourself in a mirror. If you still aren't certain, have someone observe you while you read silently. If you do read to yourself with your lips, stop. Reading makes many demands on your eyes and mind. It makes none on your lips.

4. *Failure to use reference books*

Nearly all the serious reading you do contains words, expressions, references, dates, and names that are meaningless or nearly so. This condition will apply no matter how proficient you are. So, use a dictionary. Use an atlas. Use an encyclopedia. (If you dislike interrupting your reading, make notes and look up missed items later.) Even so-called educated and experienced readers resort to such aids. They came to be "educated" and "experienced" because they consistently did just this for a long time. And if they expect to continue to be efficient readers, they won't give up the practice.

5. *Slouching and reclining*

Many people (including the author) like to read sitting in an easy chair or lying in bed. Many young readers seem to prefer reading while lying on the floor. All of us could help prevent muscular weariness and cramping if we formed the habit of doing prolonged reading while sitting erect. Good posture is also a help in correct breathing. Recline in a lounge chair, prop up in bed, or lie on the floor all you please. But when you're engaged in any sort of serious reading, don't assume any of these admittedly delightful positions.

6. *Straining your eyes*

If after concentrated reading for a short time your eyes feel tired or become red or begin to smart, something is wrong. If reading gives you a headache, it's time to seek help. Perhaps faulty posture causes these problems. Possibly the light by which you read is glaring, dim, or improperly placed. If after correcting both posture and lighting you still have difficulty, you should see an ophthalmologist or optician. It is the height of stupidity to abuse one's precious, irreplaceable eyesight. If you need eyeglasses, get and wear them.

It may be that none of the six bad habits mentioned in this chapter apply specifically to you. If not, other faulty habits do. Give this matter some consideration. Reading of all kinds will become more pleasurable and profitable without distracting and detracting reading habits. If reading continues to bother you both mentally and physically, if every time you read you feel exhausted or drained, reread Chapter 7. You cannot expect to improve your studying until you can read at times with pleasure and always without pain of mind and body.

9

Train Your Memory to Commit Itself

"I studied hard, but when I took that quiz, I couldn't remember a thing." "I knew the answer, but. . . ." "How can the teacher expect us to remember all this stuff?" "I can't say it, but it's on the tip of my tongue." "I don't remember that ever being taken up in class." "I knew it cold yesterday, but today—"

Familiar remarks, aren't they? We've heard and expressed similar ones many times. And every time we've made such a statement, we've probably wished for a better memory; for the ability to recall what we assumed we once knew; for a mind, not a sieve. You are convinced, rightly, that a better memory would help you get better grades in any course you're taking.

Like the mind, memory is not an organ of the body. It is the mental capacity to recognize previous events and experiences, the faculty to retain and revive impressions and ideas of whatever kind. When we *remember*, we "recall," or "think of again," or "keep in mind," or "remain aware of." When we *forget*, we "cease to remember," or "fail to recollect," or are "unable to recall."

Without memory, each of us would be a social and mental infant. Without the stored and shared memory of mankind, the world would be a savage wilderness.

No one possesses a perfect memory or even one that is regularly adequate. Everyone forgets. But some people apparently have better memories than others. We envy such persons and wish we could do something to improve our own. But can one improve his or her memory?

Psychologists and other students of mental processes generally agree that there is no such thing as a *bad* memory. Such a conclusion is shocking to everyone who uses his poor memory as an excuse for shortcomings and failures. It is an even greater blow to those who seem to pride themselves on their defective memories, somewhat as others are proud of their illegible handwriting. And yet there *is* such a thing as an "untrained memory." This is what everyone has who frequently lacks the ability to hold in mind what needs to be held. If your memory is not so much bad as it is untrained, how do you go about making it more efficient?

These suggestions may be useful:

1. *Make up your mind to remember.*

As with several other approaches to studying, a determination, a mental set, an act of will is essential. If you "learn" something today, thinking that surely it will be gone from your mind by tomorrow or the next day, it probably will be. You must force yourself to want to remember. The motivation for, and interest in, remembering may be to avoid embarrassment, or feel more competent and assured in performing daily tasks, or getting higher grades. Whatever it is, it must be real and apparent to you. If you are fed up with your poor memory and determined to improve it, you are on your way. It is impossible to remember things one is not interested in remembering.

2. *You must "get" something before you can "forget" it.*

When we say "I forgot" what we should be saying is "I never learned it in the first place." It is easy to get a snapshot impression of something, think we have it in mind, and fail to develop, print, and mount the picture. To remember something we must react positively and actively. We must really look, listen, stop, and think about anything we intend to get and keep in our minds. Observation and memory—close observation and good memory—go hand in hand.

Speed can be an enemy of memory, just as it can be (and often is) of reading or using a dictionary or any of several other approaches to study. You are wise, not stupid and not slow, when you take ample time to get something firmly fixed in mind. (Remember the fable of the tortoise and the hare.) If memory is an art as well as a skill, then that art depends upon the act of attention, of concentration. You can't expect to remember if you keep thinking "My mind is on something else." You can't remember unless you concentrate and take the necessary time to respond actively to what you're learning. You cannot forget something you've never really learned. Nor can you forget, except temporarily, anything you have genuinely mastered.

3. *Keep refreshing your memory.*

Everything we learn tends to fade from our minds unless we keep bringing it back into consciousness. Some event from your childhood you can recollect in every detail—provided you have thought about it enough times since it happened. But how about thousands of other happenings that must have occurred of which you have no recollection? You probably know the multiplication table perfectly, but you wouldn't if you had learned it in elementary school and totally neglected it from then on.

Memory is not a camera which, snapped once, registers a permanent image. The three *R*'s especially apply to reviewing (see Chapter 13), but they also have a direct bearing on our ability to remember: *read* (or see or do), *recite* (say to yourself or others), and *repeat* (continue the process). When reading a textbook, apply the three *R*'s to each main point. Then repeat the act after you have completed a chapter. Memory depends far more upon attention and repetition than it does upon intelligence.

4. *Organize what you want to remember.*

Experienced students of mental processes claim that the more you remember, the more you can remember. One's memory is like a muscle that can be trained, shaped, and exercised but cannot be overtrained. True, one's memory can become muscle-bound if it is required to retain numerous ideas, facts, and impressions that are unorganized and jumbled. Method (organization, outlining, structuring) may be called the "secret" of memory. William James once wrote:

> The one who thinks of his experiences most and weaves them into systematic relation with each other will be the one with the best memory.

In whatever you are studying, pick out main points—and only main points—and discard everything else. Then arrange these main points in a meaningful pattern or outline. Then, and only then, recite and repeat until you really "have" what you're trying to fix in mind. It is a misguided and hopeless practice to attempt to remember everything in an assignment or entire course of study. Select, organize, repeat—this is a time-tested, rarely failing process for remembering.

MEMORY TRICKS

Some persons have a remarkable ability to remember certain kinds of things such as telephone numbers, faces, names, dates, addresses, and the like. Others with phenomenal memories seem to rely, consciously or unconsciously, on various aids to memory. Memory experts who give public exhibitions use many and varied "tricks" to make their performances possible. It is likely, however, that most of us can improve our memories best by following the four suggestions already given.

One further comment should be made: What we remember most clearly is consciously or unconsciously associated with something known and remembered. That is, the surest means of remembering is through *association.* We are familiar with this fact: an odor "reminds" us of a place, event, or person with whom we instantly associate that odor. Some scene reminds us of something from our past. A person's face will cause us to recollect someone we knew years ago.

The memory device known as mnemonics is discussed in Chapter 23 as an aid in spelling. This aid is based on association: if you want to remember to spell *dessert* with a double *s,* associate the word with strawberry sundae and its two *s*'s. Such association, or linking, has applications other than in spelling.

For instance, if you want to remember the names of the Great Lakes, think of "homes" that dot their shores: *H*uron, *O*ntario, *M*ichigan, *E*rie, and *S*uperior. If you want to remember that you have twelve tasks to perform today, think of "month." If you need to remember that a certain river is 3365 miles long, associate its length with "year." A man whose initials are *H. L.* has no difficulty in recalling the five ingredients that he thinks make for happiness: he puts "ace" between his initials and readily recites the linked words "*h*ealth, *a*chievement, *c*ontrast, *e*xpectation, and *l*ove."

Such association, or linking, can be based on mental pictures that even appear ridiculous. On several occasions while studying U.S. history, the author attempted to learn the names of the presidents, in order. He never tried very hard and never succeeded. But several years ago, he learned them perfectly in ten minutes through a nonsense series of linkings:

> Adam (*Adams*) was the first man but the second president after *Washington.* These two had a little dog named Jeff (*Jefferson*) who went mad (*Madison*). They got their "mon" (money, *Monroe*) and took him to the vet, Dr. *Adams.* The vet took their "jack" (money, *Jackson*) and put it in a van (*Van Buren*). He then grabbed his son Harry (*Harrison*), tied (*Tyler*) him in a poke (*Polk*), and took him to a tailor (*Taylor*). The tailor's shop was filled (*Fillmore*) with stuff, but he calmly kept on piercing (*Pierce*) a buckskin (*Buchanan*) with his needle. He then got his *Lincoln* out of the garage, called his son, John (*Johnson*), and drove off without granting (*Grant*) a hello (*Hayes*) to his wife who was in the fields (*Garfield*). They picked up a boy named *Arthur* and drove toward *Cleveland,* where they stayed in the Hotel *Harrison* outside of *Cleveland.*
>
> They then set off for Mt. *McKinley,* where they saw *Roosevelt* leading a group up the slopes with fat *Taft* lumbering behind. They couldn't see *Wilson* very well because it was hard (*Harding*) to make things out in the cool (*Coolidge*) fog. So they left and went on to the *Hoover* Dam, on which they saw sitting a man with a cigarette holder in his mouth (*Roosevelt*), a true man (*Truman*), a fellow named Ike (*Eisenhower*), a youngster named Ken (*Kennedy*), and a boy named John (*Johnson*) who kept saying "nix" (*Nixon*). (Then they drove home in a *Ford.*)

Of course this sketch is silly, but time and again it has proved an infallible memory aid to the author at parties and among friends generally. It "makes no sense," but it is a method of linkage helpful in recalling a series of names. A scheme of your own composition will help you recall lists of ideas, formulas, dates, series of facts, or whatever needs recalling. Your method of linking can be sensible or nonsensical, as you please. But letting one item develop from the preceding one is an invaluable memory "trick." Try it.

A reliable memory will be an asset all your life. A good time to start developing and strengthening yours is right now when you need it in your quest for better grades. And as you work on training your memory, follow these steps:

1. Find a reasonable motive for wanting to remember.
2. Make up your mind to remember.
3. Take your time.
4. Really *see* what you look at.
5. Say it to yourself.
6. Write it in your own words.
7. Say or write it again.
8. Repeat the process.
9. Again.
10. And again.

10

Learn to Listen While Listening to Learn

Why are you regularly present in a classroom or lecture hall? You may think this question stupid and mutter something about "getting an education." But is that a good answer? Couldn't you get an education by reading, by home study, or by working at some trade or skill? Why go to the trouble, time, and cost of attending school at all?

Aside from grades and credits, you have really come to classrooms and lecture halls for the *opportunity to listen.* You will be required to do much reading and some writing, but you will listen more often than you do anything else, even talking. From infancy, most of what you and I have learned—including an ability to speak the language—has come through our ears.

For many people the time and money spent on formal education is largely wasted. Tests have proved conclusively that the majority of students remember less than half of what they hear immediately after they hear it. No matter how hard one tries to listen, even what he or she does retain gradually fades as time goes on. Further tests have shown that, after two weeks, only superior students can recall as much as one-fifth of what they heard in a class session or lecture. Yes, talking (lecturing) may be an ineffective and wasteful method of teaching, but its practice is not likely to cease any time soon.

The act of listening is a genuine skill. Learning to do it better will have a decided effect upon the grades you receive in every course you take. Like reading and writing, listening can be improved by understanding what it involves and by practicing.

Active Listening

When people talk to you, they are usually affected by how you listen. If you are attentive, you assist the speaker in saying exactly what he has in mind. Inattentiveness acts as a damper on the person talking; he will sometimes stop, or at least he will find it more difficult to express his ideas.

Try this simple experiment. In an empty room, try talking aloud to yourself about some simple fact. Your words may not flow smoothly, and you will undoubtedly become confused. Ask someone into the room and explain the same fact to him. You will find doing so far less difficult than before. We all need listeners; without them we are mentally lost as we talk.

When you are on the listening end, you have a responsibility for producing effective communication. But remember that good listening is not easily faked. Facial expressions, posture, eye movements, and gestures betray the poor listener or reveal the good one.

In the classroom, your attitude and attention can help a teacher speak more clearly and interestingly. As for grades, everyone knows that a student who appears to be listening attentively is much more likely to win a teacher's approval than one who is apparently bored and inattentive. It is also true that many a student has become at least somewhat interested in a subject once he or she began to listen and learn.

LISTENING AS A LEARNING TOOL

A friend may have a large store of knowledge to offer if you will only listen. The person who sits next to you on a bus or train or airplane may be an authority on a subject, and if you listen attentively, he or she will often pass along a wealth of information. Your school or college staff has experts in many fields; most of them will take time outside of classes to pass on what they know if they think you care. People usually are flattered and eager to share their knowledge.

Listening is sometimes a faster, more efficient means of gathering information than reading is. If you need to know something about a subject quickly, you can often find an authority on it to ask. He or she is likely to speak in terms that you can understand. The authority may also select and consolidate information from his or her broad field of knowledge to give you an accurate, generalized view of the subject; for you to do the same through reading might take weeks of research. And, of course, if you don't understand, you can ask questions for immediate clarification; as a reader you cannot question the writer so easily. Also, many times a listener can obtain valuable information not easily found in written form.

Writing that may seem dull and difficult to understand as you read it can often be understood and appreciated if you listen to it. Shakespeare's plays prove this point. They were written to be heard and are at a disadvantage when presented simply as words on a page. However, if you can first hear one of the plays, then read it, your experience is increased, with your chances of appreciating Shakespeare much better. It's not difficult to find a friend who will join you in reading aloud. If you have a record player, investigate the many available records and tapes of famous authors reading their own writings or accomplished actors reading classical literature.

Good listening is one of the best-known ways for improving language facility. Perhaps this fact stems from early childhood, when we learned to talk by listening to and imitating our elders. The principle remains valid throughout our lives. Listen to persons who are accomplished speakers, either in public speaking situations or in conversation. You will hear many such speakers; the more carefully you listen to them, the more you will be able to improve your own oral facility.

It may be obvious, but it is not stupid, to remark that the better you listen, the more you will learn. And the more you learn, the more you will be able to give back in classroom work and on papers and tests.

Listening Habits

Like everyone else, you may have picked up habits that weaken your efforts to listen while listening to learn. Once you are aware of what these faulty habits are, you can try to correct them. Do any of the following attitudes and practices affect your listening, your learning—and your grades?

1. *Supersensitive listening*

Some persons refuse to listen to anything that does not agree with their own private thoughts. Hearing statements they do not like, they immediately begin to plan a rebuttal and stop listening to what the speaker has to say. Perhaps they should make it a policy to hear the speaker out. Afterward they can make final judgments.

2. *Avoiding difficult explanations*

If something is difficult to understand, many listeners tend to give up too easily. They blame the speaker for not making his points clearer. The remedy: go out of your way to hear material that is hard to grasp. Stick with the subject from beginning to end; force yourself to listen. Listening requires practice, just as writing does.

3. *Premature dismissal of a subject as uninteresting*

If a speaker's material seems dry, some of us use that impression as rationalization for not listening. We feel that if the speaker's material is not stimulating, he must not have anything worth hearing. Yet, as someone once remarked, there are no uninteresting subjects, only uninterested people. When one forms the habit of listening attentively, many previously dull subjects seem to take on new life. Have you never become friends with, or even fallen in love with, someone you used to consider dull and uninteresting?

4. *Finding fault with a speaker's delivery or appearance*

Sometimes we become so deeply involved in a speaker's delivery or appearance that we cannot concentrate on what he or she is saying. If manner or appearance creates an unfavorable impression, we lose interest. Conversely, a speaker's looks or manner may cause fantasies that distract us with equal loss of comprehension. The most important task in listening is to learn what the speaker says, not how it is said or how he or she looks when saying it.

Listening outside School

Good listening habits can add to your store of knowledge and information outside of school as well as inside. And when you leave school, your ability to listen may become more important than ever. An adult spends at least half of his communication time listening.

That poor listeners are expensive and expendable employees is being increasingly recognized in the business world. Indeed, many of our most important affairs depend on listening. What does a jury do? It listens, sometimes to millions of words of testimony, and then makes up its mind about the case on trial. The way one votes in an election depends to a large extent upon his ability to listen.

Listening situations and opportunities confront us many times every day. What else can and should one expect in a nation that has millions of television sets, more radios than bathtubs, and several million *new* telephone installations every year?

11

Put into Your Own Words What You Read and Hear

Two effective study methods are making précis and paraphrases. Both involve work habits you have been engaged in nearly all your life. You have been making précis and paraphrases of what you read and heard ever since you entered first grade, however unaware you may have been of what you were doing.

The aim of this chapter is to provide suggestions for improving your constant use of these time-tested study practices.

The Précis

A *précis* (the form is both singular and plural and is pronounced PRAY-see) is a brief summary of the essential thought of a longer composition. It is a miniature of the original that reproduces in the same mood and tone the basic ideas of the original passage. The writer of a précis does not interpret or comment; his function is to provide a reduction of the author's exact meaning without omitting any important details.

In taking lecture notes, in doing library research, and in preparing homework assignments, you have been making and using précis for several years, perhaps without knowing or employing the term itself. (In Molière's play *The Bourgeois Gentleman* a character exclaims, "Good Heavens! For more than forty years I have been speaking prose without knowing it.") By whatever name (précis, summary, digest), the technique of condensing material is an invaluable aid.

In every reading assignment, your purpose should be to understand what the author has written, to absorb it, and to communicate it to others (especially your teacher) when requested to do so. Here are five suggestions for making précis that deserve careful study:

1. *Read the selection carefully.*

The major purpose of a précis is to present faithfully, as briefly and clearly as possible, the important ideas of the selection being "cut down." To grasp the central ideas, you must read carefully, analytically, and reflectively.

Look up the meanings of words and phrases about which you are in doubt. Do not skim, but look for important or key expressions. You must, to use Sir Francis Bacon's phrase, "chew and digest" the selection, not merely "taste" it or "swallow" it whole in a single gulp. You must see how the material has been organized, what devices the writer has used, what kinds of illustrations support the main thought. (These suggestions are, of course, those you would follow every time you concentrate on reading and thinking intelligently.)

2. *Use your own words.*

Quoting sentences—perhaps topic sentences—from each paragraph results in a sentence outline, not a précis. You must use your own words for the most part, although you may want to quote key words or phrases. Ordinarily, the phrasing of the original will not be suitable for your purposes. You are guided and aided by the order and wording of the material, but the précis itself represents your own analysis and statement of the main thought.

3. *Limit the number of words used.*

A précis must be a condensation. The length of a condensation cannot arbitrarily be determined, but most prose can be reduced by two-thirds to three-fourths. Some verse is so compact that it can be condensed hardly at all; other verse can be shortened more than good prose.

4. *Follow the plan of the original.*

In order to be faithful to your selection, preserve its proportion and order. Changing the author's plan will distort its essence. Resist the temptation to rearrange facts and ideas. Try to preserve the original mood, content, order, and tone.

5. *Use effective English.*

The condensation should not be a jumble of disconnected words and faulty sentences. It should be a model of exact and emphatic diction and clear, effective sentence construction because it must be intelligible to someone who has not seen the original. It is not likely to be so well phrased or written, but it should possess merit of its own.

The following are précis made by students. Criticize them in terms of the suggestions given above.

ORIGINAL

But as for the bulk of mankind, they are clearly devoid of any degree of taste. It is a quality in which they advance very little beyond a state of infancy. The first thing a child is fond of in a book is a picture, the second is a story, and the third is a jest. Here then is the true Pons Asinorum, which very few readers ever get over. [69 words]

—Henry Fielding

PRÉCIS

Most people lack taste; they remain childlike. Readers, like children, rarely ever get over the "bridge of asses" constituted by pictures, stories, and jokes. [24 words]

ORIGINAL

We all appear to ourselves to be thinking all the time during our waking hours, and most of us are aware that we go on thinking while we are asleep, even more foolishly than when awake. When uninterrupted by some practical issue we are engaged in what is now known as a *reverie*. This is our spontaneous and favorite kind of thinking. We allow our ideas to take their own course and this course is determined by our hopes and fears, our spontaneous desires, their fulfillment or frustration; by our likes and dislikes, our loves and hates and resentments. There is nothing else anything like so interesting to ourselves as ourselves. All thought that is not more or less laboriously controlled and directed will inevitably circle about the beloved Ego. It is amusing and pathetic to observe this tendency in ourselves and in others. We learn politely and generously to overlook this truth, but if we dare to think of it, it blazes forth like the noontide sun.

—James Harvey Robinson

PRÉCIS

Most of what we believe to be our thinking is actually *reverie*, a spontaneous process in which our ideas take a course determined by our hopes and fears, our likes and dislikes. For nothing is so interesting to ourselves as ourselves; all our uncontrolled thought concerns the Ego. Although we prefer to overlook this truth, it is self-evident.

The Paraphrase

The *paraphrase* is another type of "report on reading." The term is derived from Greek terms loosely meaning "writing [or speaking] on this model."

A paraphrase is unlike a précis in that the latter is a digest of the essential meaning of an original passage, whereas a paraphrase is a full statement of that meaning. It is a free rendering of the sense of a passage, fully and proportionately, but in different words.

The paraphrase is frequently used to make clear wording that is vague and obscure; it is a process of simplification and modernization. Each of you has read a particularly difficult poem or discussion in prose that you could not make sense of until you put it into your own words. After you did so, its meaning was clear, and you felt that you had actually translated the passage into your own thought processes.

Much of the discussion in all English and social science classrooms begins with a paraphrasing of the ideas expressed in assignments from textbooks. In other words, every student has almost daily need for reshaping source material to suit his purposes and aims. In a very real sense, much of what we say is a paraphrase of what we've read or heard.

In making (or preparing to recite) a paraphrase, follow these suggestions, which parallel those for making or writing a précis:

1. *Read and reread the original passage.*

It is impossible to properly paraphrase a passage until you have mastered its essential content, until you are familiar with its purposes, organization, and method of getting at the central idea. Just as in making a précis, read as well and think as consistently as you can. Some phrases and sentences you will probably have to reread several times, carefully and reflectively, before their meaning will come alive for you. If the passage contains obscure words and allusions about which you are in doubt, consult a dictionary or other reference book to determine meanings.

2. *Use your own words.*

Try to find understandable equivalents for words and phrases that are obscure, but do not strain for synonyms. Repeat words whose meaning is unmistakably clear; restrict your changes to passages that actually require simplifying or modernizing. For instance, the phrase *chacun à son goût* may be changed to "each to his own taste." Do not fail to make necessary changes just because it is difficult to do so.

3. *Omit nothing of importance.*

A paraphrase is a restatement and, as such, should contain the essential thought of the original in its entirety. Omitting significant detail results in distortion.

4. *Add nothing that is not in the original.*

Interpretation and explanation should be confined to making clear what the original author had in mind and should not convey the paraphraser's additional ideas. Whether you like or dislike what the writer has said, whether you agree or disagree with him, whether you think his logic is sound or faulty—these considerations do not enter into the making of the paraphrase.

To make a paraphrase does not mean that you cease to think; it means that your thinking produces a full-length statement of another's meaning.

5. *Follow the original.*

Keep as closely as clarity will permit to the form and tone of the original. If necessary, recast the passage; but be careful not to distort or to parody. Obviously, a paraphraser can hardly hope to achieve the same mood and tonal quality as the author of, say, a great poem, but he should try to preserve as much of these existing qualities as possible.

6. *Use good English.*

Any paraphrase of a good passage is worth far less than the original; but the better the paraphrase, the less the difference between it and the original. In addition to careful reading and constructive thinking, the making of a good paraphrase, just as of an effective précis, requires exact writing.

The following are paraphrases made by a student. Criticize them in terms of the suggestions given above.

ORIGINAL

On First Looking into
Chapman's Homer

Much have I travell'd in the realms of gold,
And many goodly states and kingdoms seen;
Round many western islands have I been
Which bards in fealty to Apollo hold.
Oft of one wide expanse had I been told
That deep-brow'd Homer ruled as his demesne:
Yet did I never breathe its pure serene
Till I heard Chapman speak out loud and bold:
Then felt I like some watcher of the skies
When a new planet swims into his ken;
Or like stout Cortez, when with eagle eyes
He stared at the Pacific—and all his men
Look'd at each other with a wild surmise—
Silent, upon a peak in Darien.

—John Keats

PARAPHRASE

I have read widely in the great classics of literature and have noted many examples of great poetry. I had often been told of the work of Homer and the poetry which he had created, but I never really understood or appreciated its great beauty and power until I read Chapman's translation. Then I felt as awed as some astronomer who unexpectedly discovers a new planet, or as surprised and speechless as Cortez (Balboa) and his followers were when they saw the Pacific Ocean for the first time, from Panama.

ORIGINAL

Tell me not, Sweet, I am unkind,
That from the nunnery
Of thy chaste breast and quiet mind
To war and arms I fly.

True, a new mistress now I chase,
The first foe in the field;
And with a stronger faith embrace
A sword, a horse, a shield.

Yet this inconstancy is such
As thou too shalt adore;
I could not love thee, Dear, so much,
Loved I not honor more.
—Richard Lovelace

PARAPHRASE

Do not tell me, Sweet, that I am unkind in leaving you to go to war. It is true that I now pursue a new mistress, the enemy, and that my devotion to my horse and weapons is stronger. Yet you too will approve this inconstancy, for I could not love you so much if I did not love honor more.

Learning to summarize and to rephrase what you read and hear constitute a dual step toward greater satisfaction in all study and resulting higher grades.

12

Take Notes in Précis Form

Three important causes of poor grades are (1) not taking notes in class, on lectures, and while reading; (2) taking too many notes; (3) not organizing and reviewing those notes that are taken.

Note-taking is a study skill that baffles many people. How many times have you thought to yourself "The teacher is going too fast for me to get down what she's saying" or "I'm not sure I'm getting the important points" or "I'm writing so much I must be missing a lot" or "I guess I must take poor notes because even when I can read 'em, they don't help"?

Learning to take useful notes while listening or reading is a sure step toward better grades.

Note-taking, a universal practice in all learning situations, is even more widely practiced in business and the professions. What you learn now about taking notes will be valuable to you as a homemaker, lawyer, clerk, physician, farmer, mechanic, carpenter, or in any other industry or profession.

No matter at what educational level you are, you are spending time (your own) and money (yours or someone else's) for chances to read, listen, and learn. The more efficiently you take notes, the better return you will get on your investment of time and money. This return will take the immediate form of greater satisfaction in study and higher grades for performance.

You may not need to take many notes in mathematics and related subjects, or even in applied science courses, but without good notes you will be rash to expect high grades in any of the humanities and social sciences—especially history, English, philosophy, literature, languages, and art. Also, most courses in chemistry, biology, geology, physics, and general science require note-taking.

The five suggestions following apply directly to taking notes in class and on lectures. They also apply to most reading situations as well.

1. *Provide yourself an adequate notebook.*

An astonishing number of individuals come to class without any notebook at all. If they take notes, they write on the backs of envelopes, scraps of paper, or whatever they can cadge from others. Still others use notebooks so small or messy that they have little practical value.

Equip yourself with at least one good-sized notebook, sturdily bound. A loose-leaf notebook holding sheets 8½ by 11 inches is recommended. If you prefer, use a notebook approximately the size of most of your textbooks, but don't try to use anything smaller. Insert dividers in your notebook so that notes on each subject will have their own section. Better yet, use separate notebooks for each subject you are taking. There's no law against using a pocket-sized notebook for writing down assignments, but don't try to take helpful class, laboratory, or lecture notes in a hand-sized book.

2. *Listen and think before you write.*

Many conscientious note-takers write too much. They try to cram into their notebooks everything from the teacher's opening "Good morning" to the last word uttered as the bell rings. This is stupidity, madness, or both. The right idea is never to let your pen or pencil interfere with your listening. Let both remain on your desk and pick up one or the other only when you hear something you think worth recording. Really efficient note-takers spend up to 80 percent of their time listening and thinking, and only 20 percent or less writing down summaries of what they hear. Useful notes contain the meat of a class session, not everything that was said and done. Efficient notes are a précis of a lecture or talk, not a paraphrase (see Chapter 11). Actually, good notes are full enough if they contain a précis of the *main* points of a class, not a summary of all that was said and done.

3. *Make your notes easy to read and study.*

When you write less and think more, you have time to record facts in legible handwriting (see Chapter 28) and to organize them so that they hang together (see Chapter 25). If you are using your head more than your pencil, you can jot down headings that keep related topics together. Consolidating your notes will reveal a pattern to you, not a jumble. After class, you may have to spend a few minutes organizing them, but as you become more experienced in the practice, you will find that class notes take approximately the form of an outline.

4. *Adopt your own short cuts.*

Every competent note-taker uses as many devices and tricks as he or she can to cut down on writing time. Use abbreviations as often as possible: *ex* for "example," *w* for "with," *th* for "these," "those," "them," and "that," and so forth. Any other shortened forms learned or concocted are entirely permissible, so long as they remain clear. If you know shorthand, all the better. But remember to condense, to put into précis form, even shorthand notes. Stenographic notes are usually too full and cumbersome to be helpful. Two suggestions: (1) never use any symbols or abbreviations that will be hard to decipher at a later date; (2) be inventive: concoct and master your own shortcuts.

5. *Use your notes.*

It's wasteful and silly to take notes and then ignore them. Apparently some listeners and readers take notes and, having done so, assume that nothing further remains to be done. It's also silly to think that notes should be stored away, like money in a bank, to be hauled out the night before a test or examination. Most notes become "cold" unless they are reviewed soon after they are taken. It makes good sense to read over the notes you have taken immediately after class or at least before the next session. In doing so, you can check them for completeness and clarity. If they lack both qualities, you can improve them more easily than you could weeks or months later. Also, if something seems to be missing or unclear, you can query the teacher while the topic is fresh in your mind and his. No real teacher objects to being questioned. By asking, you are indicating interest and an eagerness to learn that can hardly fail to impress.

Periodically review your notes. If a class meets three times a week, find a few minutes over the weekend to read your notes for the preceding three sessions. Or look them over after a major section of course work is covered and before another is taken up. Such reviewing will have many useful results, not the least of which is that it will reduce the amount of time needed for final review at the end of a term.

The kind of note-taking and note-use discussed thus far is

not really difficult. If you have done little or none before, you will have problems at first. But remember that although practice may not make perfect, it will surely result in improvement. As you gather experience in learning how class sessions, talks, and lectures are organized, it will become easier to organize your reports (notes) on them. The right amount of time to spend in listening and that needed for writing will become more obvious. As you become more skilled in précis-writing, you will discover your notes becoming more useful not only because they develop central ideas but also because they help you to remember through mental association the facts and figures that are in your mind because you were listening and thinking, not writing constantly. The greatest lesson to be learned about taking notes is that listening time should be converted from hypnotized stenography or placid sleep into effective learning.

Although most of what has been said thus far in this chapter applies to listening, keep in mind that reading is also listening of a sort—the kind done solely with the mind rather than the mind and ear. In reading, it is possible to follow nearly all of the suggestions made in preceding paragraphs, but a few comments can be made specifically about silent reading.

Because the material being absorbed from a textbook or other source is written, reading notes usually consist of *underlining* or *outlining*. The first practice is not strongly recommended; the second is.

Underlining is a practice of somewhat dubious value for two reasons. First, many textbooks and other reference sources are not the property of the person using them and should not be marked or defaced in any way. If the book you are reading is your own and you have found underlining a generally useful practice, go ahead. If you do, try to focus on essentials. Most students who underline tend to overdo it. Unless you concentrate on main points, you ruin the appearance of your book, suggest that everything is important (which it isn't), and waste time.

By outlining what you read (see Chapter 25) you will be providing yourself with genuinely useful material. Outlining can be done by making notes in the margin of a book (if you own it) or, better, by outline notes in your loose-leaf notebook. To this written outline you can add facts and illustrations supplied by your teacher during class time.

Many able students have found that making a précis of a section or chapter of a book is preferable to both underlining and outlining. Writing a key summary, however brief, of a portion of the book you are reading will insure that you have mastered its content. It will guarantee that you can "give it back" when required to do so in class or on a quiz. For example, here is a passage from a famous essay:

> A third kind of thinking is stimulated when anyone questions our beliefs and opinions. We sometimes find ourselves changing our minds without any resistance or heavy emotion, but if we are told that we are wrong we resent the imputation and harden our hearts. We are incredibly heedless in the formation of our beliefs, but find ourselves filled with an illicit passion for them when anyone proposes to rob us of their companionship. It is obviously not the ideas themselves that are dear to us, but our self-esteem, which is threatened. We are by nature stubbornly pledged to defend our own from attack, whether it be our person, our family, our property, or our opinion. A United States Senator once remarked to a friend of mine that God Almighty could not make him change his mind on our Latin-American policy. We may surrender, but rarely confess ourselves vanquished. In the intellectual world at least, peace is without victory.
>
> Few of us take the pains to study the origin of our cherished convictions; indeed, we have a natural repugnance to so doing. We like to continue to believe what we have been accustomed to accept as true, and the resentment aroused when doubt is cast upon any of our assumptions leads us to seek every manner of excuse for clinging to them. *The result is that most of our so-called reasoning consists in finding arguments for going on believing as we already do.* [242 words]
>
> —James Harvey Robinson, "On Various Kinds of Thinking"

After careful reading, a studen put this précis in her notebook:

> A third kind of thinking occurs when we are told that our beliefs and opinions are wrong. We may have been heedless in their formation, but our self-esteem will not permit us to change. We may have to give up, but we are not convinced. We do not study the origin of our beliefs; we believe as we have been accustomed to believe, and we seek arguments for continuing to believe as we already do. [75 words]

The student deserved, and got, an A for this condensation when it was submitted as an exercise in précis-making. She undoubtedly would have received another A had she been required to answer a question in class or on a quiz about this passage. But for practical, notebook purposes, this seventy-five-word condensation can be reduced still further. Try it.

13

View and Then Review

The best time to learn something is when you already know it. This may seem a silly remark, but it isn't. Failure to recognize and act upon this fundamental truth about learning is a major cause of low grades.

Think a minute. You read a statement or series of statements in one of your textbooks. The material is clear and understandable. You therefore go on to the next topic or close your book. How long will you remember that "learned" statement? How much of it can you recall an hour or a day or a week later? And how many times have you failed to give satisfactory answers in class or on quizzes to questions about material you had "read carefully" and had "got down cold" the night before?

Applied to studying, reviewing is the act of going over a topic or subject sufficiently to fix it in memory and be able to summarize its details. The human mind has a remarkable capacity for resisting information and an even more remarkable capacity for forgetting. It might be more accurate to say that we don't actually "forget" so much as never really learn (see Chapter 9). Learning, really learning, is not a one-time or once-over-lightly process.

Consider this incident. Many years ago, the author memorized a poem that especially appealed to him (Shelley's "Ozymandias"). He "learned" it perfectly, said it to himself a time or two, and then went about other things. Years later when the poem was mentioned in casual conversation, he volunteered to recite it. To his astonishment and embarrassment, he found that only parts of some lines came back to him. He then did what he should have done the first time: he "rememorized" the poem and said it over to himself at least once a day for a week. Following this, he recited the poem at intervals spaced over a period of months. Now he knows the poem, completely. But if he ignores it for several years, he will have to repeat the learning process.

True, in most of your studying you will be expected to memorize very little. Nor will you be required to learn every detail about a given topic. You will not be expected to remember what you have learned after the final examination is taken. Yet you will be expected at every class session to "give back," orally or in writing, comments that reveal your grasp of a subject, the more accurate and complete your comments the better. In other words, you should not count on being able to perform creditably in class or on an examination until you have "viewed" (read, heard, seen) and "reviewed" (reread, paraphrased, summarized, said to yourself).

The most valuable formula for good study is "the three *R*'s." First, one *reads*, then *recites* (says to himself or others), and then *repeats* (orally or in writing). Reading is not enough (see Chapters 7 and 8). Neither is paraphrasing (see Chapter 11). What should follow both processes is reviewing. No matter how simple and easy it is, material is rarely ever lastingly learned in one effort. Difficult matter, the sort encountered in most of your classes, requires several "learnings" at spaced intervals before it becomes firmly planted in the mind. Don't consider yourself stupid merely because you have to go over something many times. What you are doing is an important and constructive part of the process of learning. The more you playback (self-recitation), the more you will retain for present and future use.

When to Review

Most teachers, as well as the highest-ranking students in your classes, may say that the best time to review is all the time. This is not an extreme view, but it is unusual. It would be more realistic to suggest that all study should be accompanied by review and that this feedback process should occupy from one-fourth to one-third of all study time.

Specifically, after you have prepared an assignment for tomorrow's class, "say it back" to yourself. Even better, summarize in your notebook the main points of the assignment and list important facts (dates, names, formulas, and the like) that should be retained. Never assume that you "have" an assignment until you are satisfied with the playback you can write or say to yourself. And don't be too easily satisfied, either.

Another time for review comes prior to the next meeting of a class. It's an excellent idea to review the preceding session of a class to be able to link it with what's coming up. Most subjects are taught—and should be learned—in cumulative fashion. You know from experience that nearly every step in math depends upon steps previously encountered. You know that your ability to read any foreign language depends upon vocabulary that should have been mastered earlier. To a greater or lesser degree, every subject involves a series of linked and progressive steps.

Daily review of a subject should be followed by weekly review. Over weekends is an excellent time to look back over ground covered the week before. At this time you can find out if your notebook and your memory are at fault and make arrangements to replenish both at the earliest possible moment. Like a mountain climber, make certain of one step before you take another.

When the class finishes with a major topic or section of the course—a process that may require several weeks—review that section or topic before moving on to the next. If certain details or major points are not clear to you, this is the time to consult your instructor, reread your textbook, or get information from a classmate whose work is superior.

An over-all review of the entire course usually precedes a final examination. If you have reviewed your work periodically during the term, your term-end review can be accomplished quickly and easily. The top students in a class normally study less for final examinations than do mediocre or poor students—largely because they have been reviewing all along. Many teachers review work so thoroughly and constantly through questions in class and periodic quizzes that they consider final exams unnecessary. The student who has regularly reviewed his work during a term can also find cramming as unnecessary as a final exam. If he does have to face an exam, he can do so with confidence and without cramming.

This amount of suggested reviewing may seem tiresome and time-consuming. It does take time, but it will be time well spent. In addition, periodic reviewing will provide you with the satisfaction of realizing that you are constantly increasing your knowledge of a subject and gaining added confidence.

Far too many learners suffer the plight of Christopher Columbus: he didn't know where he was going, didn't know where he was when he got there, and when he got back didn't know where he had been.

How to Review

Because the subjects you are taking may vary widely, no pinpointed suggestions for reviewing can be offered. Nevertheless, here are six considerations that apply to reviewing in general:

1. The purpose of reviewing is to find out and establish the order and continuity of the daily, weekly, and monthly parts of a course. With this purpose in mind, review for significant details only—but never stop until you can see how facts fit together to form main points.

2. Passively rereading your textbook or notebook, even focusing on underlined passages in either, is not genuine reviewing. Such activity is preferable to no second glance at all, but it does not draw distinctions between what you know and what you think you know. Only when you close your book or notebook and try to say or write what you are learning will you be aware of gaps, shortcomings, and inaccuracies. Only through active feedback, oral or written, will you truly master what should be mastered.

3. Reviewing involves condensing. No one expects or wishes you to recite or write everything contained in your textbooks or that has been said or performed in class. A major contribution to education is gaining the ability to put much thought into few words. Try to summarize main points. Work within rigidly set time and space limits. Making a concise summary of a term's work is an ideal way to review for a final examination.

4. In reviewing, practice using such words as *interpret*, *illustrate*, *contrast*, *relate*, *summarize*, *evaluate*, *diagram*, and *define*. Apply them to what you are restudying. Apply them to questions you ask yourself. You can be certain that such words will be used by your teacher, who will expect you to do exactly what is called for.

5. Try to answer questions that have been suggested in class but may not have been followed up. (Some teachers throw out

such questions, intending them as helpful hints about what may later appear on tests.) Many carefully prepared textbooks contain chapter-end and section-end questions. Such questions should not be ignored when reviewing. Usually they provide definite clues to the structure and development of a topic and also highlight significant points.

6. Some subjects can profitably be reviewed in group sessions. Carefully select three or four classmates and meet in an informal but no-nonsense session to answer the questions each participant thinks may be asked on a quiz or exam. Such group meetings can turn into gabfests and bull sessions. They often do. Properly conducted, they can be enjoyable and profitable.

Systematic reviewing may strike you as a boring, overly regulated activity, one that is tedious, time-consuming, and repetitious. It may be all of these, but, even so, isn't it better than worried, frantic grubbing through masses of detail, more effective than last-minute cramming, more productive of satisfactory results than aimless reading and passive rereading?

14

Learn to Talk with People

Improving conversational ability may seem an indirect approach to better grades, but think a minute. Don't good grades largely result from (1) acquiring information and (2) communicating that information to others? Hasn't much of what you know about everything from people to places come from talks you have had with members of your family, friends, and acquaintances? Isn't talking over an assignment or test with a classmate a satisfying, time-tested method of study?

What, after all, is a question-and-answer classroom session? Teachers will unanimously agree that it is a form of conversation, a kind of dialogue involving not only teacher and student but all others in the classroom as well. The more effectively you can hold up your end of such conversations, the higher your grades are likely to be. No competent teacher is going to confuse glibness with knowledge and give you credit for being a slick talker. But few teachers will be unimpressed by your ability to speak clearly and effectively.

No quick-and-easy formula can suddenly turn you into an

effective classroom speaker. Conversation, like all other worthwhile arts, must be worked at. And it should be worked at outside school even more than in the classroom.

In daily contacts with others, occasionally try to engage in conversations that are genuine meetings of the mind—not just chatter about clothes, games, dates, the weather, records, food, movies, and television. Try to turn conversation into the stimulating pastime it should be: an honest interchange of opinions, beliefs, ideas, and facts. "Shooting the breeze" is always fun. It can be helpful and wholesome fun when it is more than mere talkativeness, superficial chitchat, and idle gossip. Many a bull session turns into a wasted evening, but some have paid classroom dividends the next day.

Talking with others—no matter who they are—will increase your own speaking abilities and, in many instances, provide you with information not available from any other source. Many people think, perhaps rightly, that they have learned more in a given course from talking with the teacher and with other students than in the classroom itself.

How can you become a good conversationalist? Here are ten suggestions concerning the act of talking with others. They can be adapted to classroom conversation in most instances.

1. Practice conversation. Join in good talk whenever you can. Listen in on good conversations when you have the opportunity to do so without being a pest or an eavesdropper. Form the habit of talking over classroom work outside class with other students or with members of your family.

2. Listen to what you consider a typical conversation between two friends. Summarize it, using direct quotations if you can.

3. Find an example of an interesting conversation in a short story, novel, or play, and analyze why you think it is interesting and effective.

4. Listen to a television or radio speaker who interests you. Prepare an analysis of this speaker's performance.

5. Carefully analyze a TV or radio interview. What is the attitude of the interviewer? of the person being interviewed? Are the questions direct, clear, and pertinent? Does the interviewee speak clearly and concisely? What does the interview accomplish, if anything? By his own attitude, questions, and comments, has the interviewer extracted information from the interviewee that is lively, useful, and informative?

6. Study every conversation you have an opportunity to overhear or engage in. Analysis of such conversations will indicate that the best talkers are those with the largest fund of interesting experiences—or, better yet, the most familiarity with subjects of greatest interest to the people in the circle. You will also observe that the best conversationalists do not talk constantly and are capable of quiet listening.

7. Listen carefully to the best conversationalist you know as he talks with someone else. What characteristics mark his performance? Has he the ability to listen as well as speak? Is his comment notable for what he says, for the way in which he speaks, or both?

8. Try to become and keep informed about subjects of timely interest: current events, political affairs, personalities in the limelight, music, sporting events, art, and literature. Read as much as you can: books, worthwhile magazines, a daily newspaper. Try to remember good stories you hear or read, funny or interesting incidents that happen to you or your friends, amusing or significant happenings you see or read about.

9. Try to find out as much as you tactfully can about any person with whom you have an opportunity to talk. For example, if you are left with the guest of honor at a reception, a stranger at a party, an older person at a dance, a teacher at a school function, don't try to interest him or her in yourself and your problems but try to draw the other person out. You probably will learn some highly interesting facts; even if you don't, your listener will not fail to be flattered by your interest and will consider you an

excellent conversationalist. A good conversationalist, as a matter of fact, is a good listener.

10. Be sincere and straightforward but also tactful, courteous, and friendly. A spirited discussion may be argumentative (a group of people will seldom agree about any matter of real consequence) but one can state opinions firmly and frankly without hurting the feelings of others, without being rude and brusque.

It requires time, thought, and patience to become a good conversationalist. But constant practice will make you less hesitant and tongue-tied than you may now consider yourself. Regular and constant interchange of thoughts and impressions with others will increase the ease and confidence of your speech. A study and analysis of your conversations with others will improve your oral classroom performance.

Even if your conversational progress is slow, keep working at it. Conversation is the most universal social activity there is. A good conversationalist is welcomed everywhere. Perhaps you already know that lack of opportunity for exchange of talk with others can lead to boredom and even produce serious mental illness—one of the most severe of all prison punishments, if not the most severe, is solitary confinement.

15

Learn to Talk to People

Learning to talk to people will affect your grades in many classes other than public speaking. Much of the talking you do, as pointed out in Chapter 14, is conversational. But numerous assignments require you to speak to an entire class, group of students, or a student assembly. In such instances, your performance will be judged, and even graded, directly or indirectly, by those who hear you—including teachers.

The way you talk tells more about you than any other activity of your life. What you say and how you say it are more revealing of your intelligence, personality, and character than the ways you dress, eat, walk, or read. Knowing how to read and write are significant accomplishments, but neither is an *essential* part of anyone's existence. Communicating with others through some sort of speech signals *is* essential.

Most people spend many school years learning to read and write, but few have ever paid much attention to learning how to talk. We have talked since infancy, and now we assume that it is as "simple" and as "natural" as breathing. It isn't.

More time, opportunities, money, and friendships are lost through careless, slovenly, inaccurate speech than through any other activity of people's lives. Because no one can speak perfectly (any more than he or she can read or write perfectly), this condition will persist. Yet everyone can learn to speak with greater confidence, fewer errors, and more genuine communication by studying his or her speech habits and giving the problem of talking to others the attention it fully deserves.

This chapter is designed to make a start in helping you get rid of any bad speech habits you may have and to confirm and strengthen you in your good ones. Improving talk is a lifelong occupation, but here are ten "commandments" that will serve as constant, never-failing guides in learning to speak effectively:

1. *Pronounce words carefully.*

More errors, inaccuracies, and misunderstandings are caused by carelessness and haste than by ignorance or inadequate vocabulary. Give speech the care and attention it deserves (see Chapter 16).

2. *Speak to be heard.*

If something is worth saying, it deserves to be heard. Don't shout, but don't mumble. Say, don't slur.

3. *Look alive.*

If you show interest in what you are saying and talk in lively tones, animation will invigorate your talk and stimulate your hearers.

4. *Take your time.*

Your tongue is slower than your mind, but it is quicker than your listener's ear. Nearly everyone speaks rapidly, drops syllables, slurs words, or runs thoughts together in headlong haste. Slow down.

5. *Learn to listen.*

Talk should be a two-way street. It is not only courteous to listen to others; learning to listen is the most effective means known to man for gathering facts, acquiring ideas—and improving speech (see Chapter 10). It is how you learned to talk in the first place. Open your ears.

6. *Vary your approach.*

The sole requirement of effective speech is that it should communicate. The tone of your voice and your choice and use of words should vary from situation to situation, from person to person. At times, your speech should be racy and pungent, at other times deliberate and formal (see Chapter 18). Talk should be appropriate. Shift gears.

7. *Be concise.*

Most statements of any kind are wordy. All of us repeat an idea in identical or similar words—and then say it again (see Chapter 21). Talk should not be cryptic and mysteriously abrupt, but it should be economical. Make it snappy!

8. *Be specific.*

Much of our speech is indefinite, not clearly expressed, uncertain in meaning. Even when we have a fairly good idea of what we wish to say, we don't seek out those exact and concrete words that would convey what we have in mind (see Chapter 19). Try to use words that have precise meaning. Don't be vague.

9. *Be original.*

It's impossible for anyone to conceive of a wholly new idea or to express an old one in fresh, original diction. And yet the greatest single error in "saying it right" is the use of trite, worn-out expressions that have lost their first vigor, picturesqueness, and appeal (see Chapter 20). Avoid clichés. Don't be a rubber stamp.

10. *Have something to say.*

With rare exceptions, people tend to talk more—and say less—than they should. After all, speech is only the faculty or power of speaking. The ability to talk is one thing; thoughts and emotions are another. Spinoza wrote that mankind would be happier if the power in men to be silent were the same as that to speak, that "men govern nothing with more difficulty than their tongues." It was a wise person who remarked at a meeting that it was better for him to remain silent and be suspected a fool than to speak and remove all possible doubt. Think first.

Keeping these ten "commandments" is within the capacity of anyone free from major speech defects. If you can keep any one of them better than you did before, you have taken a step toward improvement. If you can keep any five of them, you are an above-average speaker and your improving grades will reveal this fact.

As you study these suggestions for improving your speaking performances, keep in mind that talking and writing differ in several ways.

The speaker is usually concerned with the attention of a group, the writer with that of one individual at a time. A group is slower in getting meanings than the individual member, and the speaker must make allowances for this. Furthermore, each audience constitutes a special problem, and the speaker must take into account its size, average age, educational level, and special interests. Writing at its best is nearly universal in its appeal, but speaking is usually best when it is adapted to immediate listeners.

Oral style differs from written style. The speaker must be instantly intelligible. His hearers cannot go back and meditate on a sentence or try to figure out its meaning; if they do so, they are sure to lose what follows. The speaker's sentences as a rule are shorter and his language usually is simpler and more direct than the writer's. Reader and writer are separated, but speaker and listener are thrown into close association. An alert speaker can watch the facial expressions of his audience and thus get feedback, which is lacking in a writer–reader relationship. On the other hand, the reader is usually alone, relatively comfortable, and free from distractions, whereas the listener is physically distracted by other members of the audience. Even when he is quietly at home listening to a speech over television or the radio, it is more difficult for the listener to give close attention to it than to the printed page, which he can always reread if his attention wanders. Many more people are eye-minded than ear-minded.

The speaker's voice is an important consideration in oral communication, one that has no exact parallel in the written form. And the speaker's use of the body, which also is important in establishing communication with the audience, has no bearing whatever upon writing.

Characteristics of Good Delivery

The essential quality of good delivery is close contact with the audience. Talk *with* your listeners, not *at* them. Look straight into their eyes, not above their heads or at the ceiling or out of the window. *Be aware of them.* Don't focus on the people directly in front of you or those in the back row, but devote your attention in turn to all parts of the hall. Make each member of your audience feel you are talking directly to him.

Your manner is important. Be friendly, eager to interest, animated. Sincerity is your greatest asset. Desire above all else to make the audience like you and be interested in what you have to say.

The language of the speaker is not necessarily the language of the writer. Think of a speech as in a way an enlarged conversation, with the talking limited to one person. An effective speech must have conversational quality unless it is exceedingly formal, but it should not have what we usually think of as conversational style. That is, it should not have the careless expressions, unfinished sentences, slang, and general lack of dignity of so many conversations. Even this statement is only relative, because a pep talk at a rally before a big game may have all of these and still be a good speech if it arouses enthusiasm. In general, the language of the speech is considerably less formal than that of most prepared papers. Directness is of first importance on the platform, and it is more easily attained by shorter sentences and simpler vocabulary than the writer customarily uses. When you are before an audience, think through everything you say and say it as though you were saying it for the first time, no matter how many times you have practiced it. In other words, recreate your thoughts as you deliver them.

Your voice is important to your success as a speaker, but it is less important than your general speaking personality and your platform behavior.

Your posture will either aid or handicap you. Try to be relaxed without being sloppy, alert without being tense. Don't lean on the speaker's stand or table and don't stand first on one foot and then on the other. Learn to assume a well-poised position whenever you stand up, so that you will instinctively stand well before an audience. An easy position is one in which one foot is a little ahead of the other, with the weight centered on the ball of the forward foot. How far apart your feet should be will depend on your own height and weight—you need to establish an adequate base for your own body. If you are tall or heavy, or both, you will need a wider base than will a small, slender person. A good position will always give you a proper sense of balance. Keep your chest up, not in pouter-pigeon style but enough to give you a feeling of confidence. Keep your arms at your sides unless you are using them for gesturing, but let them hang loosely. Movement of any kind attracts notice, whereas relaxed hands are rarely noticed. If your hands are tying themselves in knots behind your back, twisting themselves in your pockets, or toying with a button, a ring, a pencil, they will distract attention from what you are saying and also add to your own nervousness. On the other hand, it isn't necessary to stand like a statue, especially if you are speaking for some minutes. No movement at all may be just as bad as constant movement. There is no reason for not moving occasionally. Hold your hands behind your back for a moment, or even put one hand in your pocket at some point. A change in position when you are making a transition from one point to another may be helpful. Above all, act alert and animated.

Don't worry about stage fright. Of course you will be frightened the first time you make a speech, even to your own class—and probably the tenth time. Many great speakers, singers, and actors never get over a feeling of panic just before making a public appearance. If you weren't a little keyed up in advance you might put forth less effort to make a successful presentation. Don't think about yourself or how you look or what the audience is going to think about you, but concentrate on your subject and your audience. Take a deep breath before you begin to speak.

Above all, don't hurry. Be sure that everyone is quiet before you begin to speak. A brief pause before beginning will afford an opportunity to size up your audience. Your speech should of course be carefully timed to meet the time limits you have been given. But don't hurry even if you think you aren't going to finish in time. Think ahead and leave out your least important point if necessary. Above all, don't rush your conclusion. Make it as clear-cut and impressive as you can, and then stop—don't go on adding remarks because you are afraid to stop. A guest lingered at the door, saying over and over to his hostess, "I'm leaving, but there was something else I wanted to say." His hostess finally said helpfully, "Perhaps it was 'goodbye.' "

Whether you are answering a question, speaking to a small group, or addressing a large audience, you make an impression of some kind on everyone who hears you. That impression will affect your grades more often and more directly than you may realize.

16

Say It Right

How can the way one pronounces words have any effect, good or bad, on grades? Think a moment. Do you speak with ease and confidence? Has a teacher ever misunderstood your answer to a question? Have you ever misunderstood a question because of the way words in it were pronounced? Can you speak, or read aloud, without fear of mispronouncing words?

Honest answers to these questions should help you realize that pronunciation has a bearing on classroom performance. If you hesitate or are afraid to speak up for fear of mispronouncing words, your grades will suffer. If you consistently mispronounce words, your teacher will be, at the least, sympathetic and, at the worst, so annoyed as to put you down as slovenly in speech and penalize you for being so.

Gaining confidence in speaking and getting rid of false ideas about pronunciation are important in all study. After all, most studying is based on words. For each of us, words actually live in oral rather than handwritten or printed form. It is a rare person who does not speak a hundred times more often than he or she writes, who does not listen more often than read. Consequently, pronunciation, the act of making the sounds of speech, is the direct, immediate, and constant concern of everyone, especially students. People spend more time speaking and listening than in any other pursuits of their lives (breathing and possibly sleeping excepted).

And yet, even if you wished to, it would be impossible for you to speak *the* English language or even "American English." Everyone's speech reflects the characteristics of a specific locality, individual background, and particular social group. Everyone learns and usually hangs on to certain speech patterns that are uniquely his own, patterns derived from the members of his family, the locality or localities in which he grew up, schools attended, acquaintances, occupation, and hobbies and recreations.

That is, no such thing as total conformity in pronunciation is possible because every speaker of a language employs his own dialect. Every pronouncer of words, no matter what his native language, has a speech pattern peculiar to him at a specific period of his life. One's individual speech pattern is known as his *idiolect*, his unique way of forming the sounds of speech. To the expert, the speech sounds of no two persons are, or ever can be, identical.

With many millions of idiolects in daily use, no way of sounding a given word can be said to be its only correct pronunciation. True, nearly everyone pronounces more than 90 percent of all words in general use in about the same way, so nearly the same that for all practical purposes the pronunciation could be called identical. Still, a trained ear would detect differences. Also, even if pronunciations of individual words seem identical, they would change and shift as they appeared in connected speech (talk, that is) because people speak at different rates and with differing emphasis on specific words.

The distinctive speech patterns of sections of the United States involve flavor and color more than substance, so that communication between speakers in different areas creates no real problem. But individual systems of pronunciation can and do exist throughout the country, no one of which can flatly be called "standard" or "universal" or "correct."

The pronunciation of any word or phrase is correct if it is one used by a majority of educated speakers in similar sets of circumstances in a particular major speech area. This definition suggests that there is more than one "correct" pronunciation for the majority of words about which differences exist.

It is a basic principle of all experts on pronunciation, including the makers of dictionaries, that the one and only test for correctness is *usage*. Rules, tradition, spelling, or word derivation may help the speaker, but they carry no weight if they differ from the accepted usage. Your problem is to pronounce words in accordance with established usage.

If you have a good ear and spend considerable time listening to speakers in person and on radio and television, you can learn the pronunciation of many troublesome words. This method of learning-by-ear has several flaws, however, among which two may be mentioned: (1) Not every effective speaker, including broadcasters and telecasters, has faultless pronunciation; (2) in any particular conversation, speech, or broadcast, you may not hear the words you wish and need to learn to pronounce.

Although no reputable dictionary is, or claims to be, an infallible guide to pronunciation, no one should ignore this source; every serious student should study one carefully. In actual fact the surest, most economical way to learn pronunciation is to consult your dictionary *when the need arises* (see Chapter 17). Do not worry about the pronunciation of any word until you read it, hear it, or anticipate the need for it in your own speech.

What such words will be must vary from person to person. No two people have the same vocabulary; no two people make the same demands on language because no two can have the same audience or identical things to say. As a conscientious individual, you will make your own list of trouble spots. Looking up words as you need to and entering them alphabetically (or by some other method that appeals to you) in your own notebook is the most efficient way to improve your pronunciation.

Every modern American dictionary presents its own system of recording pronunciation. Your first move should be to familiarize yourself with that system. Read the essay on pronunciation that every reliable dictionary contains. Study the full pronunciation key; examine the abbreviated pronunciation key at the bottom of each page or each alternate page. Only after you have taken these steps will you be able to use your dictionary intelligently as a guide in pronunciation.

Pronunciation, as you already know and as your dictionary will again inform you, depends upon the *sound* given to alphabetical letters or letter combinations and upon *accent* of emphasized syllables. The best-known set of symbols for transcribing the sounds of language is the International Phonetic Alphabet (IPA). This "alphabet," applicable to many languages, is highly accurate, but it is likely that the ordinary speaker and writer will find it somewhat cumbersome and involved.

Your most sensible approach will be to study the "pronunciation word" that appears in parentheses immediately after an entry word. It is a respelling of the word, giving the sounds of vowels and consonants, by syllables, according to the pronunciation key of the particular dictionary. As an indication of the kinds of information provided about pronunciation in your dictionary, see how it represents the varied sounds of, say, the letter *o*. You will find that the sounds of *o* are indicated by some or all of these symbols:

o—as in *odd, hot, lot, ox*
ō—as in *go, open, over, no*
ô—as in *oil, order, horn, ought*
o͝o—as in *took, book, look, poor*
o͞o—as in *pool, ooze, boot, too*

Each of the signs (symbols) appearing with words in a pronunciation key is a kind of diacritical mark. (The word *diacritical* comes from a Greek term meaning "capable of distinguishing," "distinctive.") Still other signs, or points, are occasionally added to letters to indicate a particular sound value. Among these are the *circumflex* (raison d'être); the *tilde* (cañon); *umlaut* (schön), and the *cedilla* (façade). Some dictionaries supply these and other diacritical marks with individual entries; others provide a separate key for foreign sounds. All diacritical marks are, of course, only approximations of sounds. Once you have studied the dictionary entry, try saying the word aloud. Then listen for its use in someone's speech and try it out in your own to fix the sounds firmly in your mind.

The matter of stress, or accent, is much less involved than the pronunciation of sounds, but it is important. Examine the method your dictionary employs for indicating where accents fall in given entries. Some dictionaries provide both accent marks and syllabication periods (dots) in the entry word. Others use only dots to indicate syllabication in the entry word and insert accent marks in the "pronunciation word." Learn the methods your dictionary has provided for indicating heavy (primary) stress and less heavy (secondary) stress.

When two or more pronunciations of an entry are provided, the pronunciation more generally used may or may not be given first. One reliable current dictionary shows first the pronunciation its compilers consider the one most widespread in "general American" usage. Another equally reliable dictionary lists first the pronunciation most prevalent in Eastern speech (along the North Atlantic seaboard). Any pronunciation shown in "standard," although some dictionaries do make a distinction by preceding a given pronunciation with the word *also*. Pronunciations also are sometimes labeled *British*, or *Chiefly British*, or with some other indication of regional usage.

Pronunciation, or what may be called the sound system of

language, is important, although relatively less so for the average speaker than diction or what is broadly called grammar. And yet phonology, the sound system of language, really *is* "the grammar of speech." Every user of language will find gaps in his knowledge when he encounters certain words and will be doubtful about pronunciation. The most reliable and systematic way to tackle pronunciation is consistent and informed use of a dictionary. Four other suggestions, however, may be helpful.

1. Try to form the habit of listening carefully to the speech you hear. When you hear an unfamiliar word that interests you, when you hear a pronunciation different from your own, when you hear what you think is an error in pronunciation, you should promptly haul out a dictionary. It is possible to improve pronunciation greatly just by listening, especially when one is listening to educated and informed speakers.

2. Try experimenting with listening to yourself. Many of us never *really* hear what we say. If you make a conscious effort, you can hear the sounds of your own voice and can judge its quality. You can question your accent, vowel formation, articulation, and inflection. If careful listening to your voice inhibits you from speaking (everyone becomes self-conscious at times), try recording your voice on a tape recorder. What you learn may be significant.

3. Become aware of your pronunciation without becoming frightened or overly self-conscious at your method of speaking. Remember that your primary aim should be, as H. W. Fowler wrote, "to speak as your neighbors do, not better."

4. Try to avoid the careless, slovenly, and sometimes uninformed habits of pronunciation that make nearly everyone seem less intelligent and less aware than he or she really is. Sloppy pronunciation will hurt your educational performance badly.

17

Make Friends with Your Dictionary

If you were asked what a dictionary is, you would probably answer, "It's a book that tells what words mean." It does that all right, but it is also a key that unlocks doors to much more than word meanings. In every subject you study—in junior or senior high school, in college, and in later life—it can be a guidebook to learning resources that are helpful, interesting, and even exciting.

"I already know enough words to get along with," you may say. If this is what you think, you are not entirely wrong. You *do* know the meanings, and perhaps the correct spelling and pronunciations, of several thousand words. If you did not, you would not have reached your present level of education.

No one, however, knows all the words needed to express his or her ideas and to understand all the things important in everyone's everyday life. "It was the most—er, well—." "If I could only say what I think . . ." "Don't you see what I mean?" Familiar phrases, aren't they? Never a day, hardly an hour, passes but we need to express some thought that is hard to put in words, or we read or hear some idea that we don't understand.

The reason is clear: thinking is done with words. Since we can't "keep our minds still" for long at a time, we are constantly thinking, using, hearing, or reading words. Thinking and the choice and use of words cannot be separated. In a quite real sense, no one's thinking can be better than his word supply. "A word," said a famous American writer, Oliver Wendell Holmes, "is the skin of a living thought." He was right. Deep inside, we know that he was, and we want to improve our diction (our choice and use of words) so that we can think better.

The best guide anyone can have for improving his word supply is a dictionary: a good, reliable dictionary. Make it your business to become friends with your dictionary. Few friendships you will ever form can be more rewarding. An adequate dictionary is what economists refer to as "durable goods." It can be your companion and guide for many years.

But no dictionary will help much unless you cultivate it as you would good and reliable friends. A friend is not someone you see only once in a while, or do not try to understand, or with whom you do not share experiences and from whom you do not ask advice and help. So it is with a dictionary. You should learn to understand and absorb its remarkable resources.

These three suggestions apply to all dictionary study:

1. *Get a dictionary that suits your needs.*

Avoid using a book so thin in detail and inadequate in coverage as to be little more than a guide to spelling and perhaps one or two meanings of a word. Also, obtain a dictionary that is not too heavy to use comfortably and too detailed to provide the pinpointed information needed.

Equip yourself with a sufficiently large dictionary (approximately 100,000 words) published by a reliable firm. These, for example, are good dictionaries:

The American Heritage Dictionary of the English Language (New York: The American Heritage Publishing Company; text edition, Houghton Mifflin Company)

Funk & Wagnalls Standard College Dictionary (New York: Funk & Wagnalls; text edition, Harcourt Brace Jovanovich)

The Random House Dictionary of the English Language, College Edition (New York: Random House)

Webster's New Collegiate Dictionary (Springfield, Mass.: G. & C. Merriam Company)

Webster's New World Dictionary of the American Language (Cleveland: World Publishing Company)

2. *Take your time.*

It requires only a minute to find the spelling, pronunciation, and first meaning of a word. But have you studied the entry you look up long enough to fix it in your mind? Have you really mastered the spelling, the pronunciation, and perhaps several meanings of the word? The next time you come across this word, will you have to look it up again? Have you learned enough about the entry to make it a part of your vocabulary? Time spent in thoroughly studying entries will save time and errors later (see Chapter 9).

3. *Find out how your dictionary operates.*

Discovering the spelling and one or two meanings of a word will increase your knowledge, but if you stop there you will have barely begun to take advantage of what your dictionary offers. You should learn what sorts of additional information your dictionary provides and how it presents that material.

For any word listed in a good dictionary, each of the first five of the following items of information is given. For many words, one or more of the next five kinds of information is also provided:

1. Spelling
2. Division into syllables
3. Pronunciation
4. Part(s) of speech
5. Meaning(s)
6. Level of usage
7. Origin (where the word came from)
8. Synonyms (*alike* words)
9. Antonyms (*unlike* words)
10. Other information

Only when you know how to obtain details about each of these ten items of information can you fully profit from your use of a dictionary. In addition, you need to find out how to locate this material without wasting time or effort.

With these three general suggestions out of the way, we can start at the beginning and proceed through the steps of dictionary use one at a time.

1. *The alphabet*

An alphabet is the letters of a language in their customary order. This order you have known from childhood. One of the first things learned in school or preschool days is the *ABC*'s. Knowing the alphabet is one thing, but being able to apply alphabetical order quickly and efficiently is something else. If asked where the letter *q* comes in the alphabet, you will recall that it's after the middle, but you may have to say *l–m–n–o–p–q* to find its exact place.

Practicing the alphabet and learning the approximate position of each of the twenty-six letters is a good idea because it's a timesaver. Knowing the alphabet is essential for finding words in a dictionary; knowing it thoroughly will save time and trouble. In opening a dictionary, you will know in advance about where to turn. For instance, the words beginning with *a, b, c, d* (the first alphabetical group) will occupy about the first fourth of a dictionary. By contrast, words beginning with the last four letters (*w, x, y, z*) fill about one-tenth as many pages as *a, b, c, d* words. For another tip in speeding up your use of the alphabet, remember that words starting with *m* will come almost exactly in the middle of your dictionary.

Also, keep in mind that you have to apply more than the first letter of a word to find it quickly. Both *forget* and *future* begin with *f*, but they appear pages apart, because after *f*, *o* precedes *u*, *r* precedes *t*, and so on. For instance, the alphabetical order of *premier* and *premium* is determined by the *sixth* letter; the first five letters are identical.

2. *Guide words*

Alphabetical order is helpful when you are looking for an entry, but guide words supply further assistance. Two of these so-called guide words are printed in bold black type at the top of each page of the main section of a dictionary. Assume that you are looking up the word *formerly*. Further assume that you find these guide words at the top of the page: *forlorn* and *fortify*. This means that the first entry on the page is *forlorn* and the last is *fortify*. All the other entries on the page appear in alphabetical order after *forlorn* and before *fortify*. You can tell immediately that *formerly* will be on this page because *form-* comes after *forl-* and before *fort-*. It is time-consuming and downright silly not to use guide words when consulting your dictionary.

3. *Words formed from entry words*

Sometimes the word you want does not appear as a main entry. This does not necessarily mean that the word is not in the dictionary, and you may have to do a little detective work. Actually, thousands of words do not appear as main entries. Suppose, for example, you wish to look up the spelling and meaning of *merrily* or *merriment*. Neither word may appear as a main entry, but it should not take long to figure out that these "formed words" will appear under the main entry *merry*. In any dictionary, you may discover many of the following kinds of words included *under* main entries:

1. Plurals of nouns (mystery, mysteries)
2. Comparative and superlative degrees of adjectives and adverbs (merry, merrier, merriest)
3. Principal parts of verbs (buy, bought, buying)
4. Additional words formed by a suffix added to the entry (busy, busied, busying, busyness)

4. *Spelling*

When you are looking for a word, you should (1) begin with the first letter of the word and turn to about that section of the dictionary containing that letter group. Using the guide words (2) at the top of the page you then (3) look at main entries and (4) for "formed words" at the ends of entries. If you cannot find the word you seek, it may be because you don't know how to spell it.

The dictionary can help you with an entry only after you have located it. If you have carefully followed the steps listed in the preceding paragraph and still can't find what you are looking for, it's possible that the word is not in the dictionary but more likely that you are misspelling it. If this is your problem, consult the table of English spellings given in the front of your book. You will learn, for example, that the *n* sound at the beginning of a word can be spelled in several ways: gnome, know, mnemonic, note, pneumatic.

5. *Syllabication*

In most dictionaries, a dot or period is centered on a line to indicate the division of an entry into syllables. (A syllable is a part of a word pronounced in one sound or a part of a written word corresponding to a spoken division.) For example, the word *fragmentary* is shown in four syllables: *frag·men·tar·y.* In "formed words," syllabication is indicated by periods and accent marks: *frag·men′ tal, frag′ men·tar′ i·ly, frag′ men·tar′ i·ness.* Such division is an aid in pronouncing and also in writing because it indicates places where, if necessary, a word may be broken (hyphenated) at the end of a line.

6. *Pronunciation*

Pronunciations are shown in parentheses immediately after main (**boldface**) entries. The system used in these "pronunciation words" involves letters of the alphabet combined with diacritical marks. (A diacritical mark is a point or sign attached to a letter to indicate its sound value and to distinguish it from another letter.) Take as an example the entry *divide*, followed by the pronunciation word *di·vīd′*. This device shows that the first syllable is pronounced *dih*, with the *i* sounding like the *i* in *if* or *it*. The second syllable sounds like *vaid*, with the *i* pronounced like the *i* in *ice*. Also, the accent is on the second syllable, meaning that stress in pronouncing falls here, not on the first syllable.

A short key to pronunciation is given at the foot of pages in the main vocabulary section of dictionaries. A fuller pronunciation key usually appears in front matter of the book. Study the full key as soon as you can. Refer constantly to the abbreviated key as you look up words.

7. *Parts of speech*

The eight parts of speech in the English language underlie all speaking and writing. Many of the more serious errors in language use occur because of confusion about what part of speech a word is and how that word should be used in a sentence. The part (or parts) of speech of a word are shown in italics following the pronunciation word of main entries. When more than one part of speech is entered, additional designations are run in. For example, *cold* is shown with different meanings as an adjective (adj.), adverb (adv.), and noun (n).

8. *Meanings*

In entries for words having several senses, the first definition given is usually that most frequently used. (Other definitions are listed in order of declining frequency.) Each meaning is preceded by a boldface numeral, the numbering starting again after each part-of-speech designation. Closely related meanings are defined under the same number and are set apart by boldface letters.

When you look up a word and find several meanings listed, you need to locate the right definition to fit the sense in which you found the word in reading or listening. Usually, you can tell approximately what the word must mean from the context in which it was used—that is, from words that preceded or followed it. For instance, if you read "A good baseball player, Jack left school to join a farm team," you can locate the one definition of several appearing under the entry *farm* that refers to a minor-league baseball club used by a higher league for training purposes. Definitions are given in such easy-to-understand language and are broken into different senses so fully and clearly that you should have little difficulty.

9. *Levels of usage*

Entry in a dictionary does not guarantee that a word is in good use or that special meanings of the word are appropriate in current, reputable, and nationwide use. The bulk of the English language as it is spoken and written requires no comment on its suitability, but certain words and expressions are labeled to indicate their *cultural* level—that is, their status as slang, illiteracies, informalities, and the like. Other labels are sometimes applied to suggest *geographical* areas where a given word is most common (British, Scottish, etc.); *subject* areas (fields of learning and activity such as chemistry and photography); *time of use* (archaic, obsolete, etc.); and *foreign-language* (used with words and expressions not fully naturalized into English).

10. *Origin of words*

The origin of a word, what scholars call its *etymology*, consists of facts relating to its derivation or formation. To illustrate, *etymology* is a borrowing of a French word that developed from a Latin word that was itself borrowed from Greek. The Greek word which provided the real origin of the word consists of *etymo* (true meaning) and *logos* (word).

In most dictionaries, the etymology (origin) of a word appears in square brackets after the definition(s) and before the listing of "formed words." Certain symbols and abbreviations are used in providing word origins; these appear in an etymology key inside the front cover or in front matter (introductory pages). The symbols most often used appear at the bottoms of pages in some dictionaries.

A knowledge of etymology can be useful in many ways, most notably in building vocabulary. Studying the origins of words will give you a surer sense of word meanings and can open the door to instant recognition of the meanings of related and associated words (see Chapter 18).

11. *Synonyms*

Synonyms are words that in one or more of their definitions have the same, similar, or closely related meanings. Most dictionaries contain numerous discussions of such approximately equivalent words. Studying synonyms can add richness to your vocabulary and can help you avoid using the same word over and over. The first word that comes to your mind may be the most precise and emphatic that can be chosen, but a study of synonyms may help you to choose a more exact and effective term (see Chapter 19).

12. *Antonyms*

Antonyms are pairs of words that have opposite or negative meanings: *man–beast*, *man–woman*, *man–boy*, *man–God*, and the like. A word may be an antonym of another only in a limited meaning. For example, one antonym of *man* concerns biology, another sex, another age, another religion.

Your dictionary lists or implies antonyms for many words. These "opposites" will often prove more exact and forceful terms than those that first come to mind.

13. *Other information*

Other information supplied as part of an entry or provided in separate sections in your dictionary includes numerous details discussed in preceding paragraphs. Such items, including those previously mentioned, may be listed, although not all of them appear in any one dictionary:

Principal parts of verbs
Plurals of nouns
Comparison of adjectives and adverbs
Variant spellings of words
Words spelled alike but having different meanings
Crossreferences to other entries for additional information
Listings and meanings of idiomatic expressions
Abbreviations

Examples of word use in phrases
Prefixes
Suffixes
Combining word elements
Usage notes about "correct grammar"
Foreign words and phrases
Pictorial and graphic illustrations
Capitalized words and words spelled with both capitals and small letters
A list of commonly used signs and symbols
Notes on style
Guides to punctuation and mechanics
Lists of given names
Directories of colleges and universities
Suggestions for manuscript form
Tables of weights and measures
A gazetteer and atlas

Learning and applying the efficient use of a reliable dictionary is among the most realistic steps you can take toward both achieving higher grades and enriching your entire life.

18

Increase Your Vocabulary

How often have you listened to some teacher or other speaker in a classroom or on a lecture platform and admired his or her knowledge of words? Have you ever heard someone on television or radio use words so forcefully and expertly as to incite your praise or envy? If you have never had such an experience, you are unique.

No one who has ever lived knows and uses all the words available in the English language. No one—no matter how well-educated or well-read, no matter how creative, no matter how expert in speaking or writing—fails to realize that his or her vocabulary is, at times, inexact or inadequate.

A positive and important step toward greater success in schoolwork (or almost any other kind of work) is increasing your knowledge of words so that you can speak and write more effectively and read and listen more understandingly. Some of us realize this fact, but most of us are unwilling to make a real and consistent effort to "recruit the vigor" of our vocabularies. Or, if we do make an effort, we proceed in ways guaranteed to result in failure. Looking up words occasionally in a dictionary will have no lasting effect. Sitting down in a burst of enthusiasm to memorize at random scores of words is almost valueless.

Actually, there are no easy methods of acquiring and mastering an adequate vocabulary, but gaining a vocabulary of considerable range is not so hopeless a task as you may think. A reliable scholar has revealed that even Shakespeare, that master of diction, used fewer than 17,000 words in all his plays and poems. The "average" American knows about 10,000 words—the words most common in newspapers, general magazines, and daily speaking.

Certain magazines (the *Atlantic Monthly, Harper's Magazine*) assume that their readers command the vocabulary of the "average" college graduate: 20,000 to 25,000 words. Naturally, these are not always the same words; an English major and a premedical student are quite likely to possess somewhat different vocabularies.

However, a number of careful studies have revealed that certain basic words are used most frequently in writing and speaking. One such study, Thorndike and Lorge's *The Teacher's Word Book of 30,000 Words*, contains from 10,000 to 15,000 words that are known to nearly everyone, regardless of school training. It is reasonable to assume, therefore, that you have a vocabulary of this size. With this number as a starter, you can begin to build.

Classroom work will provide many opportunities for you to double the size of your vocabulary. Words new to you appear on every page of the daily newspaper. Conversations and lectures will be full of them. Television and radio programs fill the air with them. Try to master them not only because doing so will enrich your reading, writing, and speaking, but because a good vocabulary will be important to you throughout life. A scientific investigator, Johnson O'Connor, has written:

> An extensive knowledge of the exact meanings of English words accompanies outstanding success in this country more

often than any other single characteristic which the Human Engineering Laboratory has been able to isolate and measure.

Wide reading and intelligent listening should lead straight to a good dictionary (see Chapter 17). If in reading you dislike to break the chain of thought by looking up words in a dictionary (although the very necessity for using a dictionary has already broken that chain), jot down unfamiliar words and look them up as soon as possible. Keeping a notebook nearby is a good idea. Be sure, after you have thoroughly studied a new word, to use it in speaking and writing until it is yours. Adding words to one's stock can be fascinating, but there must be a systematic and constant exercise of your will to study and use what you have acquired.

Each of us has three vocabularies. First, there is our *active*, or *speaking*, vocabulary. This is our productive word stock, the words we use daily in speech. Second, there is our *writing* vocabulary. This also is active in that we use it habitually in our writing, even though it contains some words we seldom use in speech. In addition to these two active, or productive, vocabularies, each of us has a *potential*, or *recognition*, vocabulary.

Using this potential vocabulary (the largest of the three), we can understand speakers and read and understand books, magazines, and newspapers. But in our reading and listening we encounter words we recognize and of which we have some understanding, possibly from the context, but would be unable to use in our own speaking and writing. Until we use such words, however—put them into circulation—they are not really ours.

To get words from our potential into our active vocabularies requires systematic effort, but it is the logical way to begin vocabulary improvement. Words in a recognition vocabulary already have made some impression on our consciousness; they are already partly ours. Their values, although still vague to us, can be made exact and accurate. Furthermore, quite likely they are words we shall want in our vocabularies. Probably we have come across them time and again. They are not unusual; they are words that have *use* value.

We have both to learn and to learn how to use such words before they can become parts of our active vocabularies. Try reading the current issue of one of your favorite magazines and underlining all the words that you rarely use. Then try to give a working definition of each word and to use the word in a sentence. Even the most intelligent readers usually discover when they put themselves through this test that they have simply assumed that they know words they in fact do not know. Probably a few of the words you underlined will be generally useless, but most of them will be useful ones that you can add to your working vocabulary relatively easily. Set out to master these words; move them from your potential to your active vocabulary.

Acquiring a really adequate vocabulary is, of course, a lifetime task. But it can be speeded up by wide, careful reading and attentive listening, accompanied by informed use of a good dictionary, especially study of word origins. If this counsel seems too general and too time-consuming, then turn to these three methods of learning new words in wholesale fashion:

1. *Synonyms and antonyms*

Collecting lists of synonyms and distinguishing among their meanings is an effective and often entertaining way to enlarge your vocabulary. All good dictionaries include listings and often brief discussions of hundreds of synonyms. When looking up a word, carefully study the treatment of those synonym entries that sometimes follow the definitions. If you do this, you may be able to choose a more exact and effective word for the occasion at hand and also add a useful word to your active vocabulary.

For example, after becoming aware of synonyms, will you

necessarily have to write that the girl is *cute*, the game *thrilling*, the idea *interesting*, the dress *sexy* or *mod*, the play *exciting*? A study of synonyms for *old* might add to your vocabulary these, among other words: *immemorial, aged, ancient, aboriginal, decrepit, antique, hoary, elderly, patriarchal, venerable, passé, antiquated*, and *antediluvian*.

Similarly, studying antonyms will improve your understanding and also contribute to vocabulary growth. For example, seeking antonyms for *praise* may add to your vocabulary such words as *vilify, stigmatize, lampoon, abuse, censure, blame, deprecate, condemn, impugn, denigrate, disparage*, and *inveigh against*. Even such a simple word as *join* has numerous approximate opposites, among them *uncouple, separate, sunder, unyoke, cleave, disconnect*, and *dissever*.

2. *Prefixes and suffixes*

Another method of adding to your vocabulary is to make a study of prefixes and suffixes.

A *prefix* is an element placed before a word or root to make another word of different function or meaning. (The prefix *pre-* means *before*: *pre-American, premeditate, premature.*)

Knowledge of the meanings of some of the hundreds of prefixes in English words is of enormous value in quickly getting at the sense of unfamiliar words. Following is a list of common prefixes, together with one or more approximate meanings and illustrative words:

a-	not	amoral, anonymous
ad-	to, against	adverse, adjective
ambi-	around, both	ambiguous, ambidextrous
ante-	before	antedate, anteroom
anti-	opposite	antisocial, antiwar

audio-	hearing	audiovisual, audition
bene-	well, good	beneficial, benefit
bio-	life	biography, biology
circum-	about, around	circumstance, circumflex
co-	complement of	comaker, co-signer
col-	together	collateral, collection
com-	in association	combine, compare
de-	away, down, from	demerit, degrade
dis-	apart, not, away	disbar, disability
ec- (ex-)	from, out of	eccentric, eclectic
en- (em-)	in, on, into	enact, empower
epi-	upon, before	epigram, epilogue
ex-	out of, from	exclaim, excommunicate
extra-	beyond, without	extrajudicial, extrasensory
hemi-	half	hemisphere, hemiplegia
hyper-	beyond the ordinary	hypercritical, hypersensitive
il-	not	illogical, illegitimate
im-	opposed, negative	immoral, imbalance
inter-	among, between	interdepartmental, intercollegiate
intra-	within	intramural, intravenous
ir-	not, opposed	irreligious, irreducible
meta-	along with, among	metaphysics, metamorphism
neo-	new, recent	neophyte, neolithic
para-	beside	paragraph, parachute
per-	through, thoroughly	pervert, perfect
peri-	about, beyond	perimeter, perigee
poly-	many	polygon, polysyllable
post-	behind, after	postscript, postgraduate
pro-	for, forward	proclivity, proceed
re-	backward, again	revert, return

retro-	backward	retrogress, retroactive
super-	above, beyond	supernatural, supersensitive
syn-	together, with	synthesis, syndrome
tel- (tele-)	distant	telegraph, telecast
trans-	across, beyond	transcend, transmit
ultra-	beyond, in excess of	ultraviolet, ultrasonic
un-	not, reverse of	unfair, unbend

A *suffix* is an element that is placed after a word or word root to make a term of different use or meaning. For example, the suffix *-age* has a general meaning of "belonging to." *Postage* (*post* plus *age*) has to do with a series of stations along a route that receive and send mail. With this sense of *-age* in mind, words such as *coinage*, *fruitage*, *spoilage*, and *bondage* become clear. Common suffixes include these:

-ana	Americana, collegiana
-ance	connivance, nonchalance
-dom	kingdom, freedom
-er	loiterer, embezzler
-fold	manifold, twofold
-ful	beautiful, harmful
-hood	childhood, priesthood
-ice	apprentice, novice
-ism	barbarism, plagiarism
-ity	civility, nobility
-logy	trilogy, theology
-phone	telephone, megaphone
-polis	metropolis, megalopolis
-ship	friendship, statesmanship
-some	twosome, quarrelsome
-ward	toward, afterward
-ways	always, sideways
-wise	clockwise, sidewise
-y	dreamy, infamy

3. *Combining forms*

A *combining form* is a term for a word element that rarely appears independently but forms part of a longer word. *Graph*, for example, is a combining form that appears in such words as *photograph* and *lithography*. Knowing the meanings of such forms as the following will help in increasing your vocabulary:

aqua	water	aquarium, aqualung
aristos	the best	aristocrat, aristocracy
beatus	blessed	beatitude, beatification
bios	life	biosphere, biopsy
causa	cause	causal, causation
culpa	fault	culprit, culpable
domus	house	domestic, domicile
ego	I	egoism, egocentric
facilis	easy	facile, facilitate
gramma	letter	grammar, grammatical
hostis	enemy	hostile, hostility
lex	law	legal, legalize
liber	book	library, libretto
locus	place	local, locality
mater	mother	matriarch, maternal
navis	ship	navy, navigate
pedi	foot	pedometer, pedicure
plus, pluris	more	plural, plurality
populus	people	population, populate
sanctus	holy	sanctuary, sanctify
tacitus	silence	tacit, taciturn
thermo	heat	thermometer, thermal
umbra	shade	umbrella, umbrage
vita	life	vital, vitamin

A steady increase in the size and range of your vocabulary will have a steady effect upon not only your grades but also your appreciation of all that you hear and read.

19

Say Exactly What You Mean

Just as we don't think enough about thinking (see Chapter 6), we don't think enough about diction—the choice and use of words to express what we want to say and write. The word *diction* should be familiar; it comes from a Latin word meaning "word" or "saying" and its root appears in such words as *dictionary*, *dictate*, and *dictator*. Because there are many words to choose from, because many ideas require expression in different shades of meaning and emphasis, and because errors should be avoided, diction is troublesome for all writers and speakers in and out of the classroom.

Diction should be *correct*, *clear*, and *effective*, but no standards can be absolute. Our language is constantly changing. Also, diction, like fashions in dress and food, is influenced by changes in taste. Again, what is acceptable in daily speech and conversation may not be suitable in written form. The use of this or that word cannot be justified by saying that it is often heard or seen in print. Advertisements, newspapers, magazines, and even some books exhibit faulty diction.

Common problems in choosing and using words may be summarized as follows:

1. Words should be in *current* use.
2. Words should be in *national* use.
3. Words should be in *reputable* use.
4. Words should be *exact* and *emphatic*.

A major step toward better grades is trying to make the words you employ—especially those used in papers prepared outside of class—conform to these four principles.

Current Use

The first requirement of good usage is that words must be understandable to readers and listeners of the present time. Words do go out of style and out of use. It is unlikely that you will use words not currently understood, but you should be aware of this possibility.

An *obsolete* word is one that has completely passed out of use. An *obsolescent* word is one in the process of becoming obsolete. Much slang is one or the other, as are such words as *prevent* for *precede* and *anon* for *coming*.

An *archaic* word is an old-fashioned word, one rarely used except in biblical and legal expressions: *enow* for *enough*, *lief* for *willing*, and *whilom* for *formerly*.

A *poetic* word is one occasionally used in poetry but rarely in ordinary prose or conversation: *'tis*, *'twas*, *dost*, *neath*, and *ope*.

A *neologism* is a newly coined word or phrase or an established word or phrase employed in a new meaning. Not all neologisms are contrived and artificial, but the majority are. Several well-known columnists and broadcasters repeatedly concoct neologisms. So do many sports commentators and advertising copywriters. Their productions are frequently colorful, attention-getting, and picturesque, but only a few prove permanently valuable.

Discoveries, new inventions, and occupations inspire new coinages: *A-bomb*, *rhombatron*, *realtor*, *beautician*. Registered trade names or trademarks are in the same classification: *Dacron*, *Technicolor*, *Kodak*.

New words that appear in dictionaries may have no restrictive label or be labeled "slang" or "colloquial." (Some neologisms, like *motel*, change to permanent status and become common words.) Like some slang, most neologisms are "here today, gone tomorrow." How recently have you heard or read such neologisms as *cinemaddict* (lover of films), *aristobrat* (son or daughter of rich parents), *publicator* (press agent), and *tube steak* (hot dog)?

National Use

Words and expressions understandable to us may to others be localisms, technical terms, shoptalk, or untranslatable foreign expressions. Also, idiomatic expressions acceptable in one part of the country may not be understood elsewhere. If you use such expressions as the following in speech and writing, drop them from your vocabulary, unless they are needed for some definite stylistic effect: the localisms *calculate*, *reckon*, and *guess* (for think or suppose); such semitechnical terms as *half-volley*, *eagle*, *double steal*, *full gainer*, *birdie*, *switch tacks* (unless these terms are used in direct reference to various sports); such Anglicisms as *bonnet* (hood of a car), *biscuits* (cookies), *bowler* (derby), and *lift* (elevator).

A *localism* is a word or phrase used and understood in a particular section or region. It may also be called a *regionalism* or a *provincialism*.

The western, southwestern, southern, and northeastern areas

of the United States are rich in localisms that add flavor to speech but that may not be understood in other areas. Such expressions are difficult for a native of one of these areas to detect; as a writer or speaker he accepts them as reputable and assumes them to be generally understood, since he himself has known and used them from childhood. Although such words and combinations of words may not always be explained in print, dictionaries do label or define many words according to the geographical area where they are common.

An extension of localism is *nationalism*, a term describing expressions common in or limited to English used by one of the English-speaking nations. *Americanism* and *Briticism* refer to words or word meanings common, respectively, in the United States and in the British Isles; logically, other labels might be *Canadianisms*, *Australianisms*, *New Zealandisms*, and *South Africanisms*.

Americanisms: *catsup* (tomato sauce); *levee* (an embankment); *calaboose* (prison, jail); *stump* (travel to electioneer); *bellhop*; *caboose*; *gangster*; *haberdasher*; *gusher*.

Briticisms: *accumulator* (storage battery); *tube* (subway); *croft* (small enclosed field); *petrol* (gasoline); *stay-in strike* (sit-down strike).

The specialized or technical vocabulary and idioms of those in the same work or the same way of life are known as *shoptalk*, the language people use in discussing their particular line of activity. To *talk shop* is the verb form of this expression.

Avoid introducing into writing words and expressions peculiar to, or understood only by, members of a particular profession, trade, science, or art. Legal jargon, medical jargon, and sports jargon, for example, have special meanings for people in those particular fields or occupations. So do more than forty other classifications of words that have special subject labels: *astronomy, entomology, psychology, engineering,* and so on. Examples of technical words are *sidereal* (astronomy), *broadside* (nautical), *lepidopterous* (zoology). Some have crept into popular use: *telescope* (astronomy), *virtuoso* (music and art), *stereo* (sound reproduction), *analog computer* (electronics).

Use common sense in employing *foreign words and phrases.* If the word or phrase has been Anglicized or if no good English equivalent exists, use it. But why *merci beaucoup* for "thank you" or *Auf Wiedersehen* for "goodbye"? Even *a* or *an* serves better than *per:* "$5 *an* hour." Do not use such foreign expressions merely to impress the reader.

Reputable Use

A writer's vocabulary is the *number* of words he can command; a writer's diction is the *kind* of words he uses. The first, most important, and fairest test of a word is usage. But usage must be "reputable"; that is, in diction one should follow standards set by that large body of accomplished speakers and writers who we have reason to believe know the language best. These standards rule out a number of words that most of us have in our vocabularies. In compensating for their loss, however, we may fall into errors: in substituting reputable expressions for disreputable ones, we may forget that the *primary* purpose of all writing is communication and that usage must be appropriate as well as reputable.

COLLOQUIALISMS

A *colloquialism* is a conversational word or phrase permissible in, and often indispensable to, an easy, informal style of speaking and writing. A colloquialism is not substandard, not illiterate; it is an expression more often used in speech than in writing and more appropriate in informal than formal speech and writing. The origin of the word is Latin *colloquium* (conversation). Our word *colloquy* means "speaking together"; the word *loquacious* means "given to talking, fond of talking."

Dictionary words and phrases are marked as colloquial (*Colloq.*) when the editors judge them to be more common in speech than in writing or more suitable in informal than formal discourse. A large number of words and phrases are so labeled. The term applies to many expressions because informal English has a wide range and because editors differ in interpretations of their findings. Certain contractions, such as *don't*, *shouldn't*, and *won't*, are considered "acceptable" colloquialisms; others, such as *'tis*, *'twas*, *'twere*, should be avoided even in informal writing. No objective rule or test will tell you when to use a colloquialism and when not to. In general, use a colloquialism when your writing would otherwise seem stiff and artificial.

The following are examples of colloquialisms (as in dictionaries and linguistic studies, no attempt is made to indicate their comparative rank): angel (financial backer), brass (impudence), freeze (stand motionless), don't, jinx, enthuse, phone, ad, gumption, cute, hasn't got any, brass tacks (facts), show up, try and, take a try at, alongside of, flabbergast, fizzle, flop, root for, make out, fill the bill.

You might use any or all of these colloquialisms if you are reporting the conversation of a person who would characteristically speak them. You might use one or more of them in informal writing where the tone is light or humorous or breezy. But if you use any colloquialisms at all, use only a few and be certain that they are in keeping with the purpose and tone of your writing.

SLANG

Slang is a label for a particular kind of colloquialism.

Characteristics of slang include flippant or eccentric humor; forced, fantastic, or grotesque meanings; novelty; attempts to be colorful, fresh, and vivid. Such expressions may capture the popular fancy or some segment of it (college slang, musical slang, baseball slang), but in the main they are substandard. Even so, slang may for a while be used over a broad area, and a large number of words and phrases bear the "slang" label in dictionaries. If such expressions survive, they may in time receive the respectable label "colloquial." Some of the following examples appear in dictionaries with the "slang" label; some may appear there eventually; and some will not appear at all, because their vogue is too short-lived.

> Neologisms (newly coined words): *scrumptious, wacky, shyster, mooch, beatnik, razz, oops, hornswoggle, goofy, payola, scram, nix, teenybopper, pizzazz.* (Not all newly coined words, however, are slang.)
>
> Words formed from others by abbreviation or by adding endings to change the part of speech: *VIP* (*V*ery *I*mportant *P*erson), *psych out, groovy, snafu, phony, chintzy, nervy, mod.*
>
> Words in otherwise acceptable use given extended meanings: *chicken, grind, corny, guts, lousy, swell, buck, bean, jerk, square, guy, grub, sack, blow, grease, touch, cat, fuzz, pad.*
>
> Words formed by compounding or coalescing two or more words: *whodunit, stash* (*store* and *cache*), *egghead, high-hat, attaboy* (that's the boy), *screwball.*
>
> Phrases made up of one or more newly coined words (neologisms) and one or more acceptable ones: *goof off, pork barrel, blow one's top, bum steer, shoot the bull, live it up, deadbeat, have a ball, off one's rocker, conk out, jam session, cut out, shoot the works, cool it.*

Slang, although popular, has little place in formal writing or even in effective informal writing. First, many slang words and expressions last for a brief time and then pass out of use, becoming unintelligible to many readers and listeners. Second, using slang expressions keeps you from searching for the exact words you need to convey your meaning. To refer to a person as a "creep" hardly expresses exactly or fully any critical judgment or intelligent description. Third, slang does not serve the primary aim of writing: conveying a clear and exact message from writer to reader. Finally, slang is not suitable in most formal or careful informal writing because it is not in keeping with the context. Words should be appropriate to the audience, the occasion, and the subject.

There are, however, some arguments in favor of slang in certain situations. It does express feeling. It also makes effective shortcuts in expression and often prevents artificiality in writing. Furthermore, it should be used in recording dialogue to convey the flavor of speech actually used.

IDIOMATIC USAGE

English *idiom* or *idiomatic* English concerns words used in combination with others. Of Greek origin, the word *idiom* meant "a private citizen, something belonging to a private citizen, personal," and, by extension, something individual and peculiar. Idiomatic expressions, then, conform to no laws or principles describing their formation. An idiomatic expression may violate grammar or logic or both and still be acceptable because the phrase is familiar, deep-rooted, widely used, and easily understandable—for the native-born. "How do you do?" is, for example, an accepted idiom, although an exact answer would be absurd.

A few generalized statements may be made about the many idiomatic expressions in our language. One is that several words combined may lose their literal meaning and express something only remotely suggested by any one word: *birds of a feather, blacklist, lay up, toe the line, make out, bed of roses, dark horse, heavy hand, open house, read between the lines, no ax to grind, hard row to hoe.*

A second statement about idioms is that parts of the human body have suggested many of them: *burn one's fingers, all thumbs, fly in the face of, stand on one's own feet, keep body and soul together, keep one's eyes open, step on someone's toes, rub elbows with, get one's back up, keep one's chin up.*

A third generalization is that hundreds of idiomatic phrases contain adverbs or prepositions with other parts of speech. Here are some examples: *walk off, walk over, walk-up*; *run down, run in, run off, run out*; *get nowhere, get through, get off.*

agree	*to* a proposal
	on a plan
	with a person
contend	*for* a principle
	with a person
	against an obstacle
differ	*with* a person
	from something else
	about or *over* a question
impatient	*for* something desired
	with someone else
	of restraint
	at someone's conduct
rewarded	*for* something done
	with a gift
	by a person

Usage should conform to the idiomatic word combinations that are generally acceptable. A good dictionary contains explanations of idiomatic usage following key words that need such explanation, even though interpretations of particular expressions may differ from dictionary to dictionary.

Exact and Emphatic Diction

Some (perhaps many) of the words you speak and write may be in current, national, and reputable use and yet be neither exact nor effective.

The exact use of words depends upon *clear thinking*. If we have only a vague idea, we are likely to choose for its expression the first words that come to mind. But if we know *exactly* what we have in mind, we will search for the word or words that will most accurately express what we mean to say.

For example, consider one of the overworked words in our language, *pretty*. We speak of a pretty girl, a pretty flower, a pretty day, and so on. The word *pretty* carries a somewhat general meaning and cannot be called incorrect. But does it express exactly what we mean to convey? Perhaps it would be more accurate to say that a certain girl is *attractive*, or *beautiful*, or *personable*, or *charming*, or *exquisite*, or *fair*, or *sensuous*, or *dainty*, or *engaging*. These words are not all synonyms for *pretty*, but perhaps one of them would more exactly express an impression than the now trite and ineffective *pretty*.

To determine the exact word needed, you must become aware of shades of meaning, of distinctions that clarify the idea for which you wish to use the word as symbol. When you want to describe a surface that, from every point of view, lies on a line corresponding to or parallel with the horizon, will you use *flat*, *plane*, *level*, *even*, *flush*, or *smooth*? Always choose the word that shows most exactly the meaning you intend.

Sometimes the first word that comes to mind is the most nearly exact which can be used; more often it is not. Also, remember that a word means to the reader what the reader thinks it means, not necessarily what the writer thinks.

Again, a word may be exact and yet be lacking in force, animation, and strength. It is reasonably "exact" to refer to a dog as being of *mixed breed* but more lively and emphatic to refer to it as a *mongrel.* Effective writing is vigorous and positive and uses colorless words only as necessary. Emphatic diction requires expressive nouns, verbs, adjectives, and adverbs.

The following sections are designed to help you make your writing and speech more exact *and* effective. As you study them, remember that not only may exact diction be unemphatic but that vigorous and forceful diction may be inexact.

IMPROPRIETIES

Improprieties are recognized (standard) English words misused in function or meaning. One classification of improprieties includes words acceptable as one part of speech but unacceptable as another: nouns improperly substituted for verbs, verbs for nouns, adjectives for nouns, adjectives for adverbs, adverbs for adjectives, prepositions for conjunctions. Another includes misuses of principal parts of verbs. Such improprieties have been called "coined grammar."

A word identified as more than one part of speech may be so used without question, but a word should not be moved from one part of speech and placed in another until standard usage has sanctioned this new function. Examples of grammatical improprieties:

Nouns used as verbs:	*grassing* a lawn, *suppering,* to *party, passengered,* to *suspicion,* to *suicide*

Verbs used as nouns:	*eats*, a *repeat*, a *sell*, *advise*, an *invite*
Adjectives used as adverbs:	dances *good*, *awful* short, *real* pretty
Misused verb forms:	*come* for *came*, *don't* for *doesn't*, *done* for *did*, *set* for *sit*, *of* for *have*, *seen* for *saw*, *hadn't ought* for *shouldn't*

Another classification of improprieties includes words similar to other words and used inaccurately in their place. Such words include homonyms and homographs. *Homonyms* are two words that have the same or almost the same pronunciation but are different in meaning, in origin, and frequently in spelling; for example, *real* and *reel*; *made* and *maid*; *hour*, *our*, and *are*; *accept*, *except*.

Homographs are two or more words that have the same spelling but are different in meaning, origin, and perhaps pronunciation. Examples: *slaver* (a dealer in slaves) and *slaver* (drool or drivel); *arms* (parts of the body) and *arms* (weapons); *bat* (club, cudgel) and *bat* (flying rodent). Homographs cannot cause misspelling, but they can cause confusion or ambiguity.

Near-homonyms may also cause confusion: *farther* for *further*, *father* for *further*, *genial* for *general*, *stationary* for *stationery*, *morass* for *morose*, *loose* for *lose*, *imminent* for *eminent*, *aisle* for *isle*, *allude* for *elude*, *climactic* for *climatic*.

SPECIFIC AND GENERAL WORDS

A specific word names a narrow concept; a general word names a broad concept. *House* is a general word, whereas *castle*, *chalet*, *lodge*, *mansion*, *hut*, *shack*, and *villa* are specific. A *red* dress may be *carnelian, cerise, crimson, magenta, scarlet,* or *vermilion.* A conventional verb such as *walk* is general; more specific (and occasionally more effective) are such words as *flounce, mince, prance, saunter, shamble, stagger, stride, stroll, strut, totter,* and *traipse.*

Specific words are more exact and usually more effective than general words, but writing can become overloaded with highly charged concepts. The second of the following sentences is more exact and emphatic than the first, but it is too specific to be genuinely effective.

> There was an old boat moving through the heavy sea.
>
> Like a lady wrestler among thieves, the tanker *Isobel Ann* lunged into each massive green wave and, with a grunt of ancient rage, flung the Arctic-spawned monster over her scaling brown shoulder.

CONCRETE AND ABSTRACT WORDS

A concrete word expresses something tangible, usually perceivable by one or more of the senses: *encrusted, forsythia, gargle, guillotine, lemony, waddle.* An abstract word suggests no really tangible image or impression: *duty, honor, leave, move, persuasion, slow, truth.*

Concrete words are specific, and specific words are frequently concrete; abstract words are general, and general words are often abstract. Ordinarily, and within reason, choose the specific, concrete word over the general, abstract one.

EXAGGERATION

Exaggeration is the act of magnifying, overstating, and going beyond the limits of truth. In writing, exaggeration is used to intensify or strengthen meaning: *starved* or *famished* for *hungry*, *a million thanks*, *abject adoration*.

In most instances, exaggeration actually misrepresents and is neither exact nor effective: "I thought I'd die laughing." Exaggeration occasionally may be used effectively, but it is more often misleading. Be on guard when using such words as *amazing*, *awful*, *fantastic*, *gorgeous*, *horrible*, *marvelous*, *overwhelming*, *staggering*, *terrible*, *thrilling*, *tremendous*, and *wonderful*.

AFFECTATION

Affectation is artificial behavior designed to impress others, a mannerism for effect that involves some kind of show or pretense. In language, it is evident in the use of words and expressions not customary or appropriate for the speaker or writer employing them. Getting rid of words and expressions that are not reputable and simultaneously trying to increase the vigor and appeal of one's speech and writing are worthwhile endeavors. Deliberately trying to be different or learned or impressive often results in misinterpretation, confusion, and annoyance. Pretense is a greater sin against expressive English than even "bad grammar."

For example, a recent magazine article contained this paragraph:

> The opportunity for options in life distinguishes the rich from the poor. Perhaps through better motivation, the upper levels of the poor could be tempted onto the option track. It is important to motivate such people close to breakthrough level in income because they are closest to getting a foot on the option ladder.

What this writer probably meant was "The more money you have, the more choices you have." He used reputable expressions, but he fell into the greater error of affectation.

EUPHEMISMS

A *euphemism* is a softened, bland, inoffensive expression used instead of one that may suggest something unpleasant. In avoiding the use of such nonreputable expressions as *croak, kick the bucket,* and *take the last count,* you may be tempted to write *pass away* or *depart this life.* Unless religious dictates prevent, use the short, direct word *die.* Other examples of euphemisms to be avoided: *prevaricate* for *lie, watery plain* for *sea* or *ocean, expectorate* for *spit, mortician* for *undertaker, lowing herd* for *cattle, villatic fowl* for *chicken, separate from school* for *expel, abdomen* for *belly, love child* for *illegitimate.*

Here is a short list of expressions recently noted in magazine and newspaper articles and advertisements, together with possible translations into useful English:

preowned car (secondhand car)	custodial engineer (janitor)
senior citizens (old people)	experienced tires (retreads or recaps)
problem skin (acne)	collection correspondent (bill collector)
motion discomfort (nausea)	comfort station (public toilet)
sanitary engineer (garbage man)	cardiovascular accident (stroke)

JARGON AND GOBBLEDYGOOK

Jargon is a general term sometimes applied to mixed linguistic forms for communication between speakers who do not know each other's language—for example, *pidgin English* and *lingua franca.* It refers as well to speaking and writing that contain a number of expressions unfamiliar to the general reader (the jargon of sports, the jargon of atomic physicists) and to writing filled with long words (polysyllabication) and circumlocutions (indirect or roundabout expressions).

"Short words are words of might." This observation—wise but no truer than most generalizations—does not imply that long words should never be used; it does suggest that long words are more likely than short ones to be artificial, affected, and pretentious. The user of jargon will write "The answer is in the negative" rather than "No." For him, "worked hard" is "pursued his tasks with great diligence"; "bad weather" is "unfavorable climatic conditions"; "food" becomes "comestibles"; "fire" becomes "devouring element"; "a meal" becomes "succulent viands" or "a savory repast." The jargoneer also enjoys what has been called "the trick of elegant variation": he may call a spade a spade the first time but then refer to "an agricultural implement."

It is impossible always to use concrete words, but be certain you mean precisely what you say in writing such usually vague words as *asset*, *case*, *character*, *condition*, *degree*, *factor*, *instance*, *nature*, *personality*, *persuasion*, *quality*, *state*, and *thing*. It is likely you will never really have to use such expressions as these: *according as to whether*, *along the line of*, *in connection with*, and *in regard to*.

Gobbledygook (or *gobbledegook*) is a special kind of jargon: generally unintelligible, wordy, inflated, and obscure verbiage. Jargon is always undesirable but is often understandable; gobbledygook is likely to be meaningless or quite difficult to decipher. The word was coined by a former United States congressman, grown weary of involved government reports, who apparently had in mind the throaty sound made by a male turkey.

The term is increasingly applied to governmental and bureaucratic pronouncements that have been referred to as "masterpieces of complexity." For example, the phrase "the chance of war" in gobbledygook might be "in the regrettable eventuality of failure of the deterrence policy." But gobbledygook is not confined to bureaucratic circles. Here is a direct quotation from a financial adviser concerning shares of stock: "Overall, the underlying pattern, notwithstanding periods of consolidation, remains suggestive of at least further selective improvement over the foreseeable future." What he meant: "Selected stocks will increase in price."

A plumber, an often-told story goes, wrote to inform an agency of the United States government that he had found hydrochloric acid good for cleaning out pipes. Some bureaucrat responded with this gobbledygook: "The efficiency of hydrochloric acid is indisputable, but the corrosive residue is incompatible with metallic permanence." The plumber responded that he was glad the agency agreed. After several more such letters, an official finally wrote what he should have originally: "Don't use hydrochloric acid. It eats the inside out of pipes."

Careful thought in choosing and using words is a time-consuming activity. But it is worth what it costs in time and effort. Good diction will improve your work in every class you're taking, with direct and helpful influence upon your grades.

20

Don't Be a Rubber Stamp

Conversation has been called a lost art. Perhaps it is. Many people apparently would rather watch television or turn on the radio than try to talk with others. A few people even resort to reading in preference to carrying on a conversation with someone else. Why is this?

One explanation is that we know in advance what others are going to say and even the words they will use. We expect to learn little or nothing from them and have no hope ourselves of interesting them. What they say and what we say have become "molds" of thought and expression, constantly repeated.

It's true that neither we nor anyone with whom we talk is likely to produce any really fresh, original ideas. But have you ever encountered someone who appealed to you by the way he or she spoke? Have you ever been pleased and surprised not so much by what was said as the way in which it was said? Don't some writers appeal to you largely because of the words and phrases they use to describe situations and happenings that in themselves are not especially fresh, original, or previously unknown to you?

In writing and speaking, you can make a real effort to use at least some words and phrases that are not original but are different, unexpected, or imaginative. Doing so will increase your interest in what you're communicating, keep your teacher from being bored, and improve your class standing.

This recommendation does not imply that you should strain the meanings of words or deliberately try to puzzle or shock your readers and hearers. It does suggest that you will violate neither clearness nor correctness by avoiding the overuse of words and phrases that have become stale and weary.

None of us can do this consistently. In everyday speech, in classroom recitations, and in writing of whatever kind we constantly use words that are so familiar, so much a part of us, that we cannot seem to avoid them. But in prepared talks and in papers done outside class, it's possible and advisable to look carefully and suspiciously at ways of saying things that leap into mind. It's also a good idea to remember that expressions that do not seem stale to you may be exactly that to persons, especially teachers, who have read and listened more than you have.

The tired language that everyone uses on most occasions goes by several names: triteness, hackneyed language, clichés. These words have origins that explain their meaning. *Triteness* comes from the Latin word *tritus*, the past participle of a verb meaning "to rub," "to wear out." *Hackneyed* is derived from the idea of a horse, or carriage (hackney coach), let out for hire, devoted to common use, and consequently exhausted in service. *Cliché* comes from the French word *clicher*, meaning "to stereotype," "to cast from a mold."

Trite expressions resemble slang in that both are stereotyped manners of thought and expression. Clichés may be stampings from common speech, outworn phrases, or overworked quotations.

Usually they express sound ideas (or ideas widely considered sound) and are memorably phrased. (If they were not sensible and stylistically appealing, they would never have been used so much as to become stale.) The problem with clichés is not that they are inexpressive but that they have been overused and misused to the point of ineffectiveness.

The following list of "rubber-stamp" phrases may seem long and involved. But study it carefully so as to become aware of the kinds of expressions that make speaking and writing more dull and monotonous than they need be. As you study note that (1) you have heard all, or nearly all, of these phrases; (2) you constantly use many of them; and (3) you probably can rework the ideas expressed in language that is more communicative and less trite.

absence makes the heart grow fonder
acid test
add insult to injury
age before beauty
all boils down to
all in a lifetime
all in all
all is not gold that glitters
all things being equal
all wool and a yard wide
all work and no play
along this line
apple of one's eye
apple-pie order
aroused our curiosity
as a matter of fact
as luck would have it
at one fell swoop
bark up the wrong tree
bated breath
battle of life
beard the lion in his den
beat a hasty retreat
beating around the bush
best bib and tucker
best foot forward
best-laid plans of mice and men
better late than never
better to have loved and lost
beyond the pale
bigger and better things
bitter end
blood is thicker than water
blow off steam
blow one's horn
blushing bride
blush of shame

bolt from the blue
born with a silver spoon
brave as a lion
breathe a sigh of relief
bright and early
bright future
bright young countenance
bring home the bacon
brings to mind
brown as a berry
budding genius
busy as a bee (beaver)
butterflies in (my) stomach
by leaps and bounds
caught red-handed
center of attraction
checkered career
cherchez la femme
chip off the old block
clear as mud
coals to Newcastle
cock and bull story
cold as ice
cold feet
cold sweat
come into the picture
cool as a cucumber
common, or garden, variety
conspicuous by his (her) absence
cradle of the deep
crow to pick
cut a long story short
cut the mustard
cynosure of all eyes
dainty repast
dead as a doornail
dead giveaway
deaf as a post
depths of despair
die is cast
distance lends enchantment
dog days
doomed to disappointment
down my alley
draw the line
dreamy expression
drown one's sorrows
drunk as a skunk
duck (fish) out of water
dull thud
each and every
ear to the ground
eat, drink, and be merry
eat one's hat
epoch-making
et tu, Brute
exception proves the rule
eyes like stars
eyes of the world
face the music
fair sex
far cry
fast and loose
fat as a pig
fat's in the fire
feather in his (her) cap
feathered choir

feel one's oats
festive board
few and far between
few well-chosen words
fight like a tiger
fill the bill
filthy lucre
fine and dandy
first and foremost
flash in the pan
flat as a pancake
flesh and blood
fly off the handle
fond farewell
fond memories
(a) fool and his money
fools rush in . . .
free as the air
fresh as a daisy
garden (common) variety
gentle as a lamb
get one's number
get the sack
get the upper hand
get up on the wrong side . . .
get what I mean?
gild the lily
give it a try
glass of fashion
God's country
goes without saying
golden mean
(a) good time was had by all
goose hangs high
grand and glorious
grain of salt
graphic account (description)
greatness thrust upon . . .
green as grass
green with envy
grin like a Cheshire cat
hale and hearty
hail fellow well met
hand-to-mouth
hapless victim
happy as a lark
happy pair
hard row to hoe
haughty stare
haul over the coals
head over heels
heart of gold
heartless wretch
hew to the line
high on the hog
honest to goodness
hornet's nest (stir up a)
hot as a pistol
hungry as a bear
if I had to do it over
if the truth be told
in a nutshell
inspiring sight
interesting to note
intestinal fortitude
in the last (final) analysis
in the long run
in this day and age

irons in the fire
irony of fate
it goes without saying
it stands to reason
jig is up
land-office business
last but not least
last straw
law unto himself (herself)
lead to the altar
lean and hungry look
lean over backward
leave in the lurch
leaves little to be desired
left-handed compliment
let one's hair down
let the cat out of the bag
lick into shape
like a blundering idiot
like a duck out of water
like a newborn babe
limp as a rag
little did I think
live it up
lock, stock, and barrel
mad as a wet hen
mad dash
main underlying reason
make a clean breast of
make ends meet
make hay while the sun shines
make night hideous
make no bones
make things hum
mantle of snow
many and varied
meets the eye
method in his madness
mind your *p*'s and *q*'s
missing the boat
moot question
more easily said than done
more than pleased
Mother Nature
motley crew (crowd)
must (*a* must)
naked truth
neat as a bandbox
necessary evil
needs no introduction
never a dull moment
nipped in the bud
no fooling
none the worse for wear
not to be sneezed at
number is up
of a high order
on the ball (stick)
open and shut
opportunity knocks but . . .
out of sight, out of mind
out of this world
over a barrel
ox in the ditch
parental rooftree
pay the piper (fiddler)
penny for your thoughts
pillar of society

play fast and loose
play second fiddle
play up to
point with pride
poor but honest
pretty as a picture
pretty kettle of fish
pretty penny
proud possessor
psychological moment
pull one's leg
pull the wool over . . .
pull up stakes
pure as the driven snow
put a bug (flea) in one's ear
put on the dog
rack one's brains
raining cats and dogs
read the riot act
red as a beet
ring true
rub the wrong way
sad to relate
sadder but wiser
safe to say
sail under false colors
save for a rainy day
seal one's fate
self-made man
sell like hot cakes
set one's cap for
set up shop
seventh heaven
show the white feather
shuffle off this mortal coil
sick and tired
sigh of relief
sight to behold
sing like a bird
sleep the sleep of the just
sow wild oats
start the ball rolling
steal one's thunder
strong as an ox
stubborn as a mule
stuffed shirt
take it easy
tenterhooks, be on
terra firma
that is to say
things of the past
things like that
through thick and thin
throw in the sponge
throw the book at
time hangs heavy
tired as a dog
tired but happy
tit for tat
too funny for words
too many irons in the fire
top it off
truth to tell
turn over a new leaf
view with alarm
wee small hours
wet to the skin
where ignorance is bliss

without further ado
wolf in sheep's clothing
wunderbar
you can say that again
you know
your guess is as good as mine

There's no way to get a satisfactory grade in any course unless you know the right answers. But if you do know the answers and can express them in language that is not consistently threadbare and monotonous, you have an excellent chance of raising your grades.

21

Get Rid of Deadwood

A half-century ago, stories were told about teachers who weighed papers and awarded the highest grades to those that were bulkiest and heaviest. If such rumors were ever true, they are no longer. Teachers still wish full and complete papers and answers, even in this streamlined age, but like everyone else they dislike wading through masses of words to get at the core of what is involved. Teachers know that overuse of words is a dodge to try to conceal lack of knowledge.

Nearly everyone uses more words than he needs. This overuse is especially noticeable in conversation, but many written sentences are equally guilty. Careful attention to sentence structure will usually result in a wholesale removal of words that add little or nothing to meaning or effectiveness (see Chapter 22).

Much of the most memorable writing the world has ever known is short, sharp, and word-hungry: the Golden Rule is 11 words long; the Ten Commandments take only 75 words. The most memorable speech ever delivered on this continent, Lincoln's Gettysburg Address, consists of 227 words.

Wordy Phrases and Expressions

It is a sound rule never to use two words where one will do, or twenty words where ten will serve. A speaker was once asked whether certain rules should be observed. He could have said "yes." Instead he replied, "The implementation of sanctions will inevitably eventuate in repercussions." A recent governmental pamphlet contained this monstrous sentence: "Endemic insect populations cause little-realized amounts of damage to forage and timber." What did the writer mean? Probably "Native insects harm trees and grass more than we realize."

Such writing is of course gobbledygook: inflated, pompous, and wordy. You may never be guilty of writing such highflown sentences as these, but it is likely that your work does contain numerous wordy expressions. Study the following list and check your sentences to see how many of them appear:

REDUCE THESE	TO THESE
a certain length of time	a certain time
advance planning	planning
after the conclusion of	after
as a result of	because
at the present time	now
at this point in time	now
before long	soon
by means of	by
by the time	when
come in contact with	meet
due to the fact that	since (due to)
during the time that	while
for the amount of	for
get in touch with	telephone (write, meet)
hurry up	hurry

REDUCE THESE	TO THESE
in accordance with	by
inasmuch as	since
in case	if
in connection with	with
in lieu of	instead
in order to	to
in regard to	about
in the event that	if
in the month of April	in April
in this day and age	today
in view of the fact that	since
it has come to our attention that	(begin with the word following *that*)
it is interesting to note that	(begin with the word following *that*)
I would appreciate it if	please
of an indefinite nature	indefinite
of great importance	important
on condition that	if
provided that	if
under date of May 5	of May 5
with the exception of	except

The preceding list is only a sampling of hundreds of wordy expressions that could be named.

Comb your sentences carefully to see what can be eliminated without real loss. For example, you will find that *there is* and *there are* sentences are often wordy: "In this building there are five elevators that await inspection" can do quite well without *there are* and *that.* Cutting out unnecessary words can become an interesting game, a game that will increase the effectiveness of your writing.

As a further aid in detecting wordiness, study this additional list of wordy expressions:

absolutely essential
around about that time
audible to the ear
back up
bisect in two
call up on the phone
choose up
Christmas Eve evening
combine together
complete monopoly
completely unanimous
connect up with
consensus of opinion
cooperate together
cover over
descend down
each and everyone
endorse on the back
entirely eliminated
extreme prime importance
few (many) in number
final end (outcome)
first beginnings
four-cornered square
from whence
important essentials
individual person
join together
long length
loquacious talker
many in number
meet up with
more angrier
more better
more older
more paramount
more perfect
more perpendicular
most unique
most unkindest
necessary essential
necessary need
old adage
personal friend
recur again
reduce down
repeat again
resume again
return back
revert back to
rise up
round in form
separate out
(a) short half-hour
small in size
sunset in the west
talented genius
this afternoon at 4 P.M.
this morning at 8 A.M.
visible to the eye

Reducing Predication

Reducing predication means decreasing the number of words used to make a statement. Consider these suggestions:

1. Combine two short sentences into one.

   FROM: He was a mechanic in a repair shop. He specialized in fuel adjustment.

   TO: He was a garage mechanic, specializing in fuel adjustment.

2. Reduce a compound or complex sentence to a simple sentence.

   FROM: Greta Garbo was for many years an excellent actress, and everyone admired her talent. Everyone admired the talent of Greta Garbo, who was for many years an excellent actress.

   TO: Everyone admired the talent of Greta Garbo, for years an excellent actress.

3. Reduce a clause to a phrase.

   FROM: a haze that resembled the color of smoke

   TO: a haze the color of smoke

4. Reduce a phrase to a single word.

   FROM: a haze the color of smoke

   TO: a smoke-colored haze

5. Reduce two or more words to one.

   FROM: a foreman in the Department of Shipping

   TO: a shipping foreman

Unnecessary Details

Using unnecessary details is known as *prolixity*. A prolix sentence obscures or weakens the main idea.

WORDY: Last winter the squash tournament was won by Bill Blandard with a racquet he had purchased two months before from a friend of his who had bought a new one made of catgut and who sold Bill his old one for $8.50.

IMPROVED: Last winter the squash tournament was won by Bill Blandard with a racquet he had bought from a friend for $8.50.

STILL BETTER: Last winter Bill Blandard won the squash tournament with a secondhand racquet.

Useless Repetition

The needless repetition of an idea without providing additional force or clearness is called *tautology*. This flaw is obvious in the following sentence: This entirely new and novel innovation in our program will delight our TV-viewing audience; it has just been introduced for the first time and will cause pleasure to many people who will be watching.

FAULTY: Jill was anxious for Rick to succeed and eager that he do so.
In all necessary essentials the work is completed and finished.

IMPROVED: Jill was eager for Rick to succeed.
In all essentials the work is completed.

Brevity has been called the "soul of wit." It is more than that: it is an indispensable aid in writing effective sentences. Using no unnecessary words is impossible for everyone, but eliminating most useless, space-consuming, time-wasting words and expressions constitutes a major step toward better writing. It is also a direct way to receiving better grades on what you write and say.

22

Take Seven Steps to Better Sentences

Everything we say or write depends upon that basic unit of thought, the sentence. Your reports, research papers, answers to many examination and test questions, memos, and personal and business letters are phrased in sentences. Improvements in the quality of sentences should result in corresponding grade improvement.

Talking about the qualities of sentences is an artificial activity. Actually, good sentences are as much a matter of personality and judgment as of rules and requirements. Good sentences will come when you know what you want to say, have some interest in what you know or think, and need to share that knowledge and understanding with your reader.

Naturalness and ease should be primary goals in sentence writing, but it will help to review the major characteristics of good sentences. A sentence should be correct, clear, and effective. These somewhat vague and general qualities can be pinpointed.

1. *Sentences should be complete.*

Since the word *sentence* can mean "a stated opinion," all groups of words that "make sense" to a reader or listener can be called sentences. A complete, sense-making statement should (1) have a subject and a predicate either stated or clearly implied; (2) not begin with a connecting word (*although, before, while,* etc.) unless an independent clause follows in the construction.

Avoid setting off a phrase as a sentence.

My final year in school I studied hard every night. *Getting ready for college entrance tests.*
(The italicized phrase is not complete; attach it to the sentence which precedes it or add to it words that will make it a sentence: "I was getting ready for college entrance tests.")

Avoid setting off a dependent clause as a sentence.

Although the course is difficult. You should be able to handle it.
(Omit "although" and capitalize "the" *or* substitute a comma for the first period and thus join the two clauses.)

2. *Sentences should be properly punctuated.*

A sentence can also be defined as a group of words that begins with a capital letter and ends with a period. It should not be joined to another sentence without any punctuation or with inadequate punctuation. Two sentences run together are said to be "fused"; two joined by only a comma result in a "comma fault."

FUSED: Spending money is easy my allowance is gone almost before I realize it.

COMMA FAULT: Spending money is easy, my allowance is gone almost before I realize it.
(This "sentence" contains two independent statements. Write each as a separate sentence, or place a semicolon—or colon—between them.)

3. *Words in sentences should appear in proper order.*

An effective English sentence is composed of words arranged in patterns. That is, a word may have one meaning in one position, another meaning in another, and no meaning at all in still another position. Related words should be kept together so that readers may see their connection. Modifiers, especially, should not be misplaced or allowed to dangle; closely related parts of a sentence should not be split.

Misplaced modifier:
We saw the car strike the telephone post with our own eyes.
(Place the last four words at the beginning of the sentence, in which position they will be connected with the word they modify, *we*.)

Dangling modifier:
While working last night, the lights went out.
(Insert in the dangling phrase a needed subject and verb, or revise the main clause: "While I was working last night, the lights went out." "While working last night, I was suddenly plunged into darkness.")

Squinting modifier:
The mechanic who charges honestly *from the point of view of a car owner* is worthy of praise.
(The italicized phrase "looks both ways," or "squints," be-

cause it can refer to what precedes or what follows it. Place the phrase at the beginning of the sentence or at the end, depending upon meaning.)

Split construction:

Whenever possible, logically related elements should be kept together. Splitting verbs in a verb phrase, dividing the two parts of an infinitive, and placing something between a preposition and its object usually result in awkwardness or confusion.

This building has, *although it is difficult to believe,* been struck three times by lightning.
(Place *has* and *been* together: "Although it is difficult to believe, this building has been . . ." or "This building has been struck . . .")
He asked us to *as soon as possible* leave the room.
(Move the italicized words to the end of the sentence.)
Jennifer crept into, *although she was terrified*, the darkened room.
(Place *into*, a preposition, next to its object, *the darkened room*, by moving "although she was terrified" to the beginning or end of the sentence.)

4. *Sentences should be logical in structure.*

Structure involves grouping words with other words or word formations (phrases, clauses). An illogical construction refers to a grouping which (1) is contrary to reason, (2) violates some principle of regularity, (3) fails to make good sense, (4) omits an important word or words, (5) adds an element that has no grammatical function, or (6) substitutes a dependent clause functioning as one part of speech for another.

A writer can expect his readers to give careful attention but not to untangle mixed and illogical constructions such as the following:

Omission of necessary words:

I never have and undoubtedly never will write good letters. (The word *written* should be added after *have.*)

That teacher has interest and regard for our welfare. (Add *in* after *interest.*)

Your performance was the greatest success. (Revise to read: "Your performance was the greatest success of any achieved thus far" *or* "Your performance was a great success." The latter revision completely removes the cause of the error, an incomplete comparison.)

Confusing blends:

Illogical blends often creep into language. *Regardless* and *irrespective* cannot logically be blended into *irregardless. In spite of* and *despite* should not be merged into *despite of*. Blending *where* and *at which* results in a faulty sentence such as "Where does he live at?" *or* "The town where I live in is quite small."

Mixed or double comparisons:

A confused construction may occur when a writer includes two comparisons in the same statement. A second comparison should appear only after the first has been completed.

The battle of Gettysburg was one of the greatest if not the greatest single conflict of the Civil War. (Revision: "The Battle of Gettysburg was one of the greatest single conflicts of the Civil War, if not the greatest.")

Double negatives:

Speech is filled with such expressions as "haven't scarcely" and "can't help but." Try to avoid double negatives not because "two negatives make a positive" (they do not), but because they are unacceptable in general use. "I didn't get none" and "I didn't see nobody" are clear in intent and meaning but are illiterate; "not scarcely enough" and "not hardly any" are not illiterate but are unacceptable.

Adverbial clauses as nouns or noun substitutes:

A dependent clause functions as a particular part of speech. Do not use an adverbial clause in place of a noun, noun phrase, or noun clause.

> Stealing is *where* (is *when*) one takes the property of another without permission. ("Stealing is the act of taking property without permission.")
> My high fever was *because* I was in a weak condition. ("My weak condition caused my high fever.")
> *Because* she had no new dress was the reason Millie stayed at home. ("Millie stayed at home because she had no new dress.")

Faulty parallelism:

When two or more ideas in a sentence are related in purpose, they should be presented in the same grammatical structure: words, phrases, clauses.

> Ned hoped that he might earn a good reputation and to make a lot of money. ("Ned hoped that he might earn a good reputation and that he might make a lot of money," or use two infinitives, "to earn" and "to make.")
> That TV production was beautiful, lively, and had an exciting plot. ("That TV production was beautiful, lively, and exciting.")

Faulty coordination:

Inaccurate, illogical, or excessive coordination gives readers hazy or incorrect impressions of the relationships of ideas and their relative degrees of significance.

Inaccurate: Jim wanted to go to the dance, *and* he had to study. (Use *but*, not *and*.)

False: This is a beautiful tennis court, *and which* we enjoy using. (Supply a preceding "which" clause: "This is a beautiful tennis court which is well cared for and which we enjoy using." Better, cut out deadwood: "We enjoy playing on this beautiful tennis court.")

Run-on: My family bought a new color TV set, and it was a beauty, and it had a big screen. ("My family bought a beautiful new TV color set with a wide screen.")

Faulty subordination:

When a writer emphasizes one idea in a sentence he automatically subordinates others. If he doesn't, his sentences will come out in primer style like those of children just learning to talk. Ability to distinguish a main idea from a subordinate one is a sign of maturity.

Upside-down: We were getting tired of walking, when we saw an approaching car. ("When we were getting tired of walking, we saw an approaching car.")

Excessive: I liked to watch the children who fed the squirrels the nuts which were on sale on the corner stand that was near the park entrance. ("I liked to watch the children who fed nuts to squirrels in the park." If you wish to include mention of the nut stand, do so in a separate sentence.)

5. *Sentences should be consistent in structure.*

Consistency in a sentence means that its parts are in agreement and should so remain without shifts in tense, subject and voice, number, person, or class of pronouns.

Tense:
She was walking along the street when a Honda turned the corner; it *careens* wildly as if its rider *is* unconscious. (Change *careens* to *careened*, *is* to *were*.)

Subject and *Voice*:
Join the Navy and the world will be seen—through a porthole. ("Join the Navy and see the world—through a porthole.") That is, make *you* (understood) the subject of both verbs; put the verbs in the active voice.

Number:
If a student really studies hard, they are bound to succeed. (Change *they* to *he* and *are* to *is*, or pluralize both subject and verb in the first clause: "If students really study . . .")

Pronouns, person, and *class*:
If one really studies hard, you will usually succeed. (*One* is an indefinite pronoun in the third person; *you* is a personal pronoun in the second. ("If you really study hard, you will usually succeed" *or* "If one really studies hard, he . . .")

6. *Sentences should be unified.*

A sentence may be both long *and* unified, but it should neither ramble nor contain unrelated ideas. A sentence should express one thought or a group of closely related thoughts.

Mary wore a new dress, and she had a good time at the party. (The new dress may have contributed to Mary's "good time," but the two parts of the sentence are logically unrelated. Revision: "Wearing a new dress and a radiant smile,

Mary was the most sought-after girl at the party, where naturally she had a good time.")

7. *Sentences should be concise.*

A sentence such as "My slowness in adding and subtracting had the effect of making my boss regret the decision that led him to hire me" can be shortened to "My slowness in arithmetic made the boss regret hiring me." A phrase such as "are of the opinion" can be shortened to "believe." "At the present time" usually means "now" (see Chapter 21).

Reducing predication:

Reducing predication involves decreasing the number of words used to make a statement. Two sentences sometimes can be combined; some clauses can be shortened to phrases; some phrases may be reduced to single words.

We gazed at the sky which had the color of amber. ("We gazed at the amber-colored sky.")
She was a teacher in the field of mathematics. ("She was a mathematics teacher.")

Numerous other suggestions and devices for making sentences more correct, clear, and effective could be mentioned. But concentration on only these seven steps to better sentences will dramatically improve their quality—and your resulting grades.

23

Spell It Right

You know whether you are a good speller, a so-so speller, or a poor speller. Your teachers know, too, and not only those who teach English. Although spelling is usually considered a part of English training, many instructors in other subjects are quick to note spelling errors, and some will penalize or criticize you for making them.

You can argue, with some reason, that a science or math or history teacher should grade your work only for what it reveals. Some teachers do, some don't. The latter follow the prevailing tendency of society to penalize misspellings. The one thing demanded of everyone who has had educational advantages is the ability to spell. Fairly or unfairly, rightly or wrongly, misspelling is a frequently accepted sign of illiteracy.

The main reason for this somewhat illogical and possibly unfair reliance on spelling as an index of intelligence and literacy is that correct spelling is the one fixed and certain thing about our language. The overwhelming majority of words are spelled in one way. All other ways are wrong. The accepted system is accepted.

You can vary your choice of words as much as you please. You can use different sentence structures. You can unnecessarily split an infinitive or use a double negative without being thought wholly illiterate. But you can spell most words in only one correct way. Most of your teachers have learned to spell and, like many other members of society, will consciously or unconsciously penalize you if you haven't.

If spelling were more difficult than it is, the problem would be solved. Then few of us could spell correctly and nearly everybody would be bad spellers together. But enough people—including most schoolteachers and college instructors—have learned to spell correctly to make things difficult for those who can't. This is the situation now and we must accept it.

At some future time, correct spelling may be thought unimportant. Until then, a sensible course of action is to realize that spelling can be learned like any other discipline and that if we wish to be considered educated and literate we'd better get busy.

The first and most important step toward correct spelling is to have the desire to learn, really to want to become a competent speller. The second is to devote the necessary time to learn. The third is to use all available means to learn.

Remember these words of an experienced teacher of spelling: "All investigations indicate that any *child* of normal intelligence can learn to spell with little difficulty in a reasonable length of time." Other spelling authorities assert that the common causes of poor spelling are *carelessness* and *laziness.*

Most people are not, by birth and constitution, chronic misspellers, but many do have trouble with spelling. In addition to desire, time, and means, it helps to realize that spelling correctly is not an impossible problem.

Perhaps you feel disturbed by your spelling errors and have a sufficient spelling conscience to do something about it. Or perhaps you are among those who doubt their ability to master this difficult subject. You may have tried many times and failed. If so, is there any hope for you?

The answer is that if you really have a desire to learn to spell perfectly you can, provided:

1. You can pronounce such words as *advise* and *advice* so that they will not sound exactly alike.
2. You can look at such words as *rain* and *rein* and in a single glance, without moving your eyes, detect the difference between them.
3. You can sign your name without looking at the paper on which you are writing and without even consciously thinking about what you are doing.
4. You can tell your friend Joe from your friend Bill by a mere glance.
5. You can learn a simple rhyme, such as "Old King Cole was a merry old soul . . ."
6. You can remember that there is a "ball" in "balloon" or that "business" is no "sin."
7. You can learn the alphabet, if you do not know it already.
8. You can equip yourself with a reliable dictionary.
9. You can learn what a syllable is and proofread your writing syllable by syllable.
10. You have normal intelligence, here defined as the ability to read and write simple English and come in out of the rain.

If you can honestly meet these ten provisions, you can learn to spell *without ever making a mistake.* If you can pass Number 10 and only three or four of the others, you can still double your spelling efficiency. It's worth trying, isn't it?

There is no *one* best method of learning to spell correctly.

What works for you may not work for someone else, and vice versa. But six approaches are effective, one or more of which may work for you. Learning to spell is an individual matter, so that one of these methods is certain to be more helpful than others. Here are the six approaches:

1. Mentally see words as well as hear them.
2. Pronounce words correctly and carefully.
3. Use a dictionary.
4. Learn a few simple rules of spelling.
5. Use memory devices.
6. Spell carefully to avoid errors.

1. *Words should be seen as well as heard.*

The ability to visualize words, to see them in the mind's eye, is the hallmark of the good speller. When a word is mentioned, a proficient speller can "see" the word in full detail, every letter standing out, as though it were written down before him. Here is a method of learning to see words mentally:

1. With your eyes on the word being studied, pronounce it carefully. If you don't know the proper pronunciation, consult a dictionary.
2. Study each individual letter in the word; if the word has more than one syllable, separate the syllables and focus on each one in turn.
3. *Close your eyes* and pronounce and spell the word either letter by letter or syllable by syllable, depending on its length.
4. Look at the word again to make certain that you have recalled it correctly.
5. Practice this alternate fixing of the image and its recall

until you are certain that you can instantly "see" the word under any circumstances and at any time.

Such a procedure is especially valuable when dealing with tricky words that add or drop letters for no apparent reason, that contain silent letters, or that transpose or change letters without logical cause: *explain*, but *explanation*; *curious* but *curiosity*; *proceed* but *procedure*; *maintain* but *maintenance*; *pronouncement* but *pronunciation*; *fire* but *fiery*.

The most frequent error in visualizing words is mistaking one word for another to which it bears some resemblance: *accept* and *except*; *adapt* and *adopt*; *affect* and *effect*; *all together* and *altogether*; *beach* and *beech*; *breath* and *breathe*; *council* and *counsel*; *formally* and *formerly*; *its* and *it's*; *loose* and *lose*; *statue*, *stature*, and *statute*; *urban* and *urbane*; *want*, *wont*, and *won't*; *yolk* and *yoke*.

Literally thousands of "look-alikes" and "sound-alikes" such as these suggest that you try to become visual-minded.

2. *Pronounce words carefully and correctly.*

Spelling consciousness, an awareness of words, depends in part on correct pronunciation. Properly pronouncing the following words will help some people spell them correctly; mispronouncing them will cause nearly everyone spelling trouble: *carton*, *cartoon*; *celery*, *salary*; *color*, *collar*; *concur*, *conquer*; *dingy*, *dinghy*; *elicit*, *illicit*; *finally*, *finely*; *gig*, *jig*; *minister*, *minster*; *pastor*, *pasture*; *plaintiff*, *plaintive*; *sink*, *zinc*; *specie*, *species*; *tenet*, *tenant*.

Here are seven specific suggestions to keep in mind:

1. Do not add vowels or consonants in pronouncing such words as *athletics*, *disastrous*, *height*, and *similar*, and you

will not misspell them as "ath*a*letics" or "ath*e*letics," "disast*e*rous," "height*h*," and "simil*i*ar."

2. Do not omit consonants in pronouncing such words as *environment, February, government,* and *library.*
3. Do not omit syllables in pronouncing *accidentally, criticism, laboratory, miniature, sophomore.*
4. Carefully examine words that contain silent letters: *subtle, muscle, pneumonia, psychology, handsome, would, solemn, listen,* and many, many others.
5. Watch the prefixes of words: *perform* and *perhaps* (not *preform* and *prehaps*), *prefix* (not *perfix*), *proposal* (not *porposal*).
6. Beware of words containing lightly stressed syllables: *dollar, grammar, mathematics, professor.* Exaggerate the trouble spots: *dollAr, grammAr, mathEmatics, professOr.*
7. Form the habit of pronouncing and spelling troublesome words syllable by syllable, writing them, and then pronouncing them aloud in order to relate the sound to the spelling.

3. *Use a dictionary.*

When you are doubtful about the spelling of any word, you should check it immediately in your dictionary. You should not, however, have to spend half your writing time flipping pages of the dictionary rather than communicating. Intelligent use of a dictionary can help prevent trouble. That is, certain approaches to the vast amount of knowledge recorded in a dictionary can fix helpful principles and patterns in your mind so that you do not have to consult it for, at most, more than 5 percent of the words you use. Certain facts about word derivations, prefixes, suffixes, plurals, apostrophes, hyphens, and capitalization can be learned easily—facts that apply to large numbers and classes of words and that help to improve your spelling in wholesale fashion (see Chapter 17).

4. *Learn a few simple rules of spelling.*

If you happen to study carefully a number of words with similar characteristics, you can make some generalizations about their spelling. In fact, observers have been doing just this for more than a century, with the result that fifty spelling rules have been formulated.

Generalizations about the groupings of letters that form classes of words do help some people spell more correctly. The five basic rules given below are of particular value in spelling correctly certain classes of words:

Words Containing *ei* or *ie*

About 1000 fairly common words contain *ei* or *ie.* It helps to know that *ie* occurs in about twice as many words as *ei,* but the problem is not thereby fully solved. The basic rule may be stated in this well-known verse:

Write *i* before *e*
Except after *c*
Or when sounded like *a*
As in *neighbor* and *weigh.*

This rule, or principle, applies only when the pronunciation of *ie* or *ei* is a long *e* (as in *he*) or the sound of the *a* in *pale.*

Here is another way to summarize the rule and its reverse: When the sound is long *e* (as in *piece*) put *i* before *e* except after *c.* When the sound is not long *e* (as it is not in *weigh*) put *e* before *i.*

Still another way to state the principle is this: When the *e* sound is long, *e* comes first after *c*, but *i* comes first after all other consonants: ceiling, conceit, conceive, deceit, perceive, receipt, achieve, aggrieve, cashier, chandelier, handkerchief, hygiene, reprieve, retrieve.

This much of the rule is fairly simple. The last two lines of the verse refer to words in which *ei* sounds like *a*. Fortunately, only a few everyday words, such as the following, fall in this group: chow mein, eight, feint, freight, heinous, neighbor, reign, veil, vein, weight.

A few words are exceptions to this basic *ei–ie* rule or are not fully covered by the verse. The best advice is to learn the following words by some method other than trying to apply the rule, which doesn't work: either, Fahrenheit, fiery, financier, height, leisure, neither, protein, seize, sleight, stein, weird.

Final *e*

Hundreds of everyday words end in *e*, and thousands more consist of such words plus suffixes: *care, careful, hope, hopeful.* In our pronunciation nearly all *e*'s at the ends of words are silent: *advice, give, live.* Actually, the usual function of a final silent *e* is to make the syllable long: *rate* but *rat*, *mete* but *met*, *bite* but *bit*, *note* but *not*.

Final silent *e* is usually dropped before a suffix beginning with a vowel but is usually retained before a suffix beginning with a consonant.

advise, advising
amuse, amusing, amusement
argue, arguing
arrive, arrival
bare, barely, bareness
believe, believable
care, careful, careless
desire, desirable
dine, dining
excite, exciting
extreme, extremely
ice, icy
like, likable
love, lovable
move, movable
owe, owing

purchase, purchasing	use, usable, useless
safe, safely, safety	value, valuable
sincere, sincerely	whole, wholesome

This basic rule is clear enough, but it does not cover all words ending in silent *e*. Here are additions and exceptions to the general principle:

Silent *e* is retained when *ing* is added to certain words, largely to prevent them from being confused with other words.

dye, dyeing, to contrast with *die, dying*
singe, singeing, to contrast with *sing, singing*
tinge, tingeing, to contrast with *ting, tinging*

Silent *e* is retained in still other words before a suffix beginning with a vowel. Sometimes this is done for the sake of pronunciation, sometimes for no logical reason at all: *acre, acreage*; *cage, cagey*; *courage, courageous*; *here, herein*; *mile, mileage*; *service, serviceable*; *shoe, shoeing*; *there, therein.*

Final *y*

Words ending in *y* preceded by a consonant usually change *y* to *i* before any suffix except one beginning with *i*: *angry, angrily*; *beauty, beautiful*; *carry, carries, carrying*; *dignify, dignified, dignifying*; *happy, happier, happiness*; *lucky, luckier, luckily*; *marry, married, marriage*; *pity, pitiful, pitying.*

Words ending in *y* preceded by a vowel do not change *y* to *i* before suffixes or other endings: *annoy, annoyed, annoyance*; *betray, betrayal, betraying*; *buy, buyer, buying.*

Here are some everyday words that follow neither part of the "final *y*" principle: *baby, babyhood*; *busy, busyness*; *day, daily*; *lay, laid*; *pay, paid*; *say, said*; *shy, shyly, shyness*; *wry, wryly, wryness.*

Doubling Final Consonant

Most words of one syllable and words of more than one that are accented on the last syllable, when ending in a single consonant (except *x*) preceded by a single vowel, double the consonant before adding an ending beginning with a vowel. This is a complicated rule but a helpful one, as may be seen: *admit, admitted*; *drop, dropped*; *forget, forgettable*; *occur, occurred*; *plan, planning*; *run, running*. Several important exceptions, however, should be noted: *transfer, transferable*; *gas, gases*. Note, also, that the rule applies only to words accented on the last syllable: *refer, referred*, but *reference*; *prefer, preferred*, but *preference*.

"One-Plus-One" Rule

When a prefix ends in the same letter with which the main part of the word begins, be sure that both letters are included. When the main part of a word ends in the same consonant with which a suffix begins, be sure that both consonants are included. When two words are combined, the first ending with the same letter with which the second begins, be sure that both letters are included. Here are some examples: *accidentally, bathhouse, bookkeeping, cleanness, cruelly, dissatisfied, irresponsible, meanness, misspelling, overrated, really, roommate, suddenness, underrate, unnecessary, withholding*.

The only important exception to this rule is *eighteen*, which, of course, is not spelled "eightteen." Also, keep in mind that three of the same consonant are never written solidly together: *cross-stitch*, not "crossstitch"; *still life* or *still-life*, not "stilllife."

5. *Use memory devices.*

One kind of memory device has the rather imposing name of *mnemonics*. The word is pronounced "ne-MON-iks" and comes from a Greek word meaning "to remember." A *mnemonic* is a special aid to memory, a memory "trick" based on what psychologists refer to as "association of ideas," remembering something by associating it with something else. You have been using mnemonics most of your life (see Chapter 9).

A mnemonic will be most helpful when you base it upon some happening or some person in your life. That is, you must invent, or use, only mnemonics that have a *personal* association of ideas.

Here are a few examples of mnemonics. They may not help you because they have no personal association, but they will provide ideas for the manufacture of your own:

all right: Two words. Associate with *all correct* or *all wrong*.
argument: I lost an *e* in that *argument*.
believe: You can't *believe* a *lie*.
compliment: A compl*i*ment is what *I* like to get.
corps: Don't kill a live body of men with an *e* (corpse).
February: *February* makes one say "Br."
piece: Have a *piece* of *pie*.
potatoes: *Potatoes* have eyes and *toes*.
together: To - get - her.
vaccine: Va*cc*ine is measured in *c*ubic *c*entimeters (*cc*'s).

6. *Spell carefully to avoid errors.*

When writing, you concentrate on what you are trying to say and not on such matters as grammar, punctuation, and spelling. This concentration is both proper and understandable. But in your absorption you are quite likely to make errors of various sorts, including some in spelling, that result from haste or carelessness, not ignorance.

Since many English words really are difficult to spell, we should be careful with those we actually know; yet it is the simple, easy words nearly everyone *can* spell that cause over half the errors made. Listed below are twelve words or phrases repeatedly found misspelled. They are so easy that you are likely to look at them scornfully and say, "I would never misspell any one of them." The fact is that you probably do misspell some of these words on occasion, or other words just as simple.

a lot, *not* alot	research, *not* reaserch
all right, *not* alright	Spanish, *not* Spainish
doesn't, *not* does'nt	surprise, *not* supprise
forty, *not* fourty	thoroughly, *not* throughly
high school, *not* highschool	whether, *not* wheather
ninety, *not* ninty	wouldn't, *not* would'nt

Learning to spell is an individual matter. One attack on correct spelling will work for one person but not for another. Perhaps it would be more precise to say that although certain words cause trouble for a majority of people, any list of commonly misspelled words will contain some that give you no difficulty and omit others that do. The best list of words for you to study is the one you prepare yourself to meet your own needs and shortcomings.

Once again, correct spelling is less important than many other subjects. But "spelling it right" is a significant step toward better grades.

24

Punctuate It Right

Punctuation may strike you as playing an indirect, superficial, and unimportant role in a quest for better grades. It doesn't. Everyone who reads anything you write will be conscious of punctuation or will be unconsciously affected by it. A misplaced decimal point (actually a period) will mar a grade in math. An omitted comma or period or other mark of punctuation may cause a social studies teacher to misread a sentence and fail to give you credit for what otherwise would be a satisfactory answer.

Correct punctuation is not mechanical and arbitrary. It is *organic*. It belongs to, and is a part of, everything you write. If you doubt that punctuation is an integral part of writing, ask a friend or classmate to copy ten lines from a newspaper, magazine, or book, omitting all marks of punctuation. Then read what he or she has copied. You may be able to make sense of it, but how much time and effort did it cost you?

Because correct punctuation is itself a form of communication, it's unreasonable to expect a teacher not to be affected by writing that is faulty or inadequate in punctuation. The meaning and purpose of words and their relationships to each other are often entirely dependent upon punctuation.

If you are still unconvinced of the importance of punctuation, think about how you speak.

When you talk, you do not depend on words alone to tell your listener what you mean. The tone and stress of your voice affect the meanings of the words you use: you speak calmly or angrily; you whisper or yell; you lower or raise your voice. Facial movements and bodily gestures add meanings to words; you grin or grimace, nod or shake your head, wiggle a finger, shrug a shoulder, raise an eyebrow, wink, move your hands, or lean backward or forward.

The true meaning of conversation is affected by pauses and halts that sometimes are as significant as words themselves. Nearly everyone has seen a skilled actor on television or in films convey moods, ideas, and emotions without uttering any words at all.

When you write you are "talking" to someone who is not there. In writing, you "speak" across space and time to your readers. Your statements, questions, pauses, emphases, and emotional states must be suggested by marks of punctuation.

The needs of the eyes are different from those of the voice and ear, but the primary aim of every mark of punctuation is to make writing clear. In fact, this is the one and only true aim of punctuation: making unmistakable the meaning of written words.

Punctuation may seem a complex, involved, and difficult problem, but it will appear easier if you break it down to its basic purposes. All punctuation has four, and only four, aims:

1. Ending
2. Introducing
3. Separating
4. Enclosing

1. To *end* or *terminate* a statement—use a period, question mark, or exclamation point.

It's beginning to rain.
Is Mother home?
How nice to see you!

2. To *introduce*—use a comma, colon, or dash.

He asked only one thing, respect.
His goal was simple: to succeed in business.
My purpose is simple—success.

3. To *separate* parts of a sentence or word—use a comma, semicolon, dash, hyphen, or apostrophe.

If you must go out in this weather, please drive carefully.
Some people enjoy tomato juice at breakfast; I find it unappealing.
Sneezing, wheezing, and coughing—these are symptoms of the common cold.
Susan Ludlow was elected secretary-treasurer.
It is almost eleven o'clock.

4. To *enclose* parts of a sentence or a whole section—use commas, dashes, quotation marks, single quotation marks, parentheses, brackets. Enclosure marks are used in pairs, except when the capital letter at the beginning of a sentence takes the place of the first or when a terminating mark at the end takes the place of the second.

An elderly lady, Miss Jane Russell, was my favorite grade school teacher.

Miss Jane Russell, an elderly lady, was my favorite grade school teacher.

My favorite grade school teacher was Miss Jane Russell, an elderly lady.

You are not—and everyone around here knows it—a very careful driver.

You are not a careful driver—and everyone around here knows it.

"The word 'lousy' is not in reputable use as a term in literary criticism," said the lecturer.

You are referred to the United States Constitution (see especially Article VII).

The article began: "People these days are to [*sic*] busy to think about problems that arise more than 100 miles from their homes."

You are already familiar with the dozen most important marks of punctuation. Look them over:

.	Period	,	Comma
?	Question mark	;	Semicolon
!	Exclamation point	:	Colon
—	Dash	" "	Double quotation marks
-	Hyphen	' '	Single quotation marks
'	Apostrophe	( )	Parentheses

You have seen each of these marks thousands of times. You have used all of them, or nearly all, many times. Think of them as what they are: shorthand devices or road signs calculated to help the reader along his way.

Closely related to punctuation is the matter of *mechanics.* This rather vague term applies to the use of capital and small letters, italics (underlining in longhand or typing), abbreviations, and the writing of numerals. Principles governing the use of mechanics are less involved and easier to learn than those of punctuation. But they, too, are important if your written work is to receive the highest grades possible.

Ideally, you should punctuate as little as you can without making your work unclear and illogical. A tightly knit style requires a minimum of punctuation. But be certain that whatever punctuation you do use is logical, correct, and an organic part of what you are writing.

25

Divide and Conquer

As a small child, you probably spent hours every day playing with blocks. It was fun to arrange them in different ways, knock them down, and start over again. Certain of your childhood toys had parts that could be removed and replaced. As you grew older, you may have become fascinated by puzzles that could be solved by placing pieces together in certain ways. In all such play, you were learning to put items in order, a process you have continued all your life.

As you prepare for bed tonight, you may recall the events of your day. You may run through it from start to finish or put together the specific happenings connected with social affairs, or sports, or classroom work. You will be "putting the day in order," trying to reconstruct what has been a jumbled pattern of events and experiences. And later, as you lie in bed, awaiting sleep, you may look forward to tomorrow, planning what you will do at given times.

You may not think of such mental activity as outlining, but that is what it is—the practice (and habit) of putting things in place and in perspective. But outlining is more than mechanical activity. It is essential in the thought patterns of everyone who does not want his or her life to be disordered and chaotic. Learning to outline the tasks, opportunities, experiences, and rewards of daily living is centrally important in your development as an individual and as an improving student.

Preparing outlines develops an ability to distinguish between what is important ("first things first") and what is unimportant. Outlining helps train the mind to be orderly. It teaches you how to plan an approach to a class assignment, an afternoon of fun, an examination, a business conference, a sports event, or whatever.

An outline need not be detailed, elaborate, or constructed according to a rigidly formal scheme. It may consist of some notes lodged only in your mind. It may be a rough and hurriedly penciled sketch. Nor, having prepared an outline of some sort, are you required to follow it slavishly. It should be your servant, not your master. But because few, if any, of us think logically, we need some control over random ideas and plans that pop into our heads. Arranging clusters of related ideas in sensible sequence is what outlining is all about.

You should prepare some kind of outline for each answer to an essay question on an examination, for a talk, a composition, a research paper—or any project that develops a series of ideas, facts, and opinions. Such an outline should provide (however sketchily and inadequately) some structure giving form to what you are going to write or say.

The plan for a formal outline has become standardized. Although not always needed, such an outline is unvaryingly constructed in this form:

I. Main topic
    A. Subtopic
    B. Subtopic

II. Main topic
    A. Subtopic
    B. Subtopic
    C. Subtopic
        1. Subtopic under C
        2. Subtopic under C
            a. Subtopic under C 2
            b. Subtopic under C 2

The scheme just set forth is only a plan. Of course it does not mean that every outline must contain two main headings or two subtopics under the first main heading, and so on. It does indicate the correct scheme for handling main ideas and subheadings in whatever number and order they logically occur.

Three kinds of formal outlines are available for use: *topic*, *sentence*, and *paragraph*.

TOPIC OUTLINES

Consisting of words and phrases, a topic outline is the simplest and usually most helpful of all outlines. Here, for instance, is a sample topic outline for a paper (or talk) on one's first day at a new job:

MY FIRST DAY AT WORK

I. Sleeplessness the night before
II. Early morning preparation
III. The trip to work
IV. Getting started
V. How the day went

Such a scheme is really a "sketch" outline, but it may be made more elaborate. In fact, the expanded outline that follows could contain five or six main heads instead of the two shown.

I. Prework jitters
   A. The night before
      1. Setting the alarm clock
      2. Sleeplessness
      3. Thoughts of failing
   B. The next morning at home
      1. Hurried dressing
      2. A bolted breakfast
II. The workday
   A. Getting to work
      1. A run for the bus
      2. My nervousness and other riders' composure
   B. The first hour
      1. Meeting the foreman
      2. Inability to understand
      3. Helpfulness of another worker
      4. Gradual easing of tension
   C. How the day went
      1. Slow passage of time
      2. Lunch hour
      3. Afternoon exhaustion
      4. Quitting time
      5. Satisfied feeling
      6. Readiness for tomorrow

Sentence Outlines

A sentence outline consists of complete sentences, not words and phrases. It is likely to be clearer to the writer than a topic outline and is more helpful to a reader who wishes to make useful suggestions.

For illustrative purposes, here is how Part I of the topic outline previously given could appear in a sentence outline:

MY FIRST DAY AT WORK

I. I was nervous and jittery the night before I was to begin work.
   A. I set the alarm clock and turned in early.
   B. I could not get to sleep and tossed restlessly.
   C. My mind was tortured with fears of not being able to do the job.

II. The next morning I was tired and still nervous.
   A. I dressed hurriedly and clumsily.
   B. I did not feel like eating but bolted my breakfast.

Paragraph Outlines

A paragraph outline consists of groups of sentences (perhaps mainly topic sentences) indicating the contents of entire paragraphs. Such an outline may be used in planning your own composition, but it is even more helpful in setting down summary sentences to indicate the thought of successive paragraphs in a selection being studied.

In the paragraph outline, material is not classified into major headings and subheadings; rather, the topic of each paragraph is simply listed in the order in which it is to appear. For illustration, here is a specimen paragraph outline of a part of the topic outline previously shown:

1. Dashing from the breakfast table, I made a run for the bus.
2. My inner fears and worries had me in a turmoil, but other riders on the bus seemed calm and even casual.
3. The foreman was gruff, and my worries increased.
4. My hands were sweaty and my knees felt weak so that I couldn't catch on to what I was supposed to do.

5. A man nearby saw my confusion and kindly showed me, slowly and clearly, what my job was.
6. As I began to catch on, my hands stopped sweating and I began to feel easier in mind and body.
7. The morning passed slowly, and I thought lunchtime would never come.
8. During the afternoon, my muscles grew more and more tired, and I had to hang on until quitting time.
9. A I walked to catch the bus home, I felt satisfied that I had met the test of the first day and could meet the challenge of the next without fear.

Correct Outline Form

Any outline that clearly reveals structure is effective, so that "correctness" in form is more often a matter of convention than of logic. Writers, however, have tended to follow certain conventions.

1. Outlining is division; subdivision means division into at least two parts. If a single minor topic (subhead) must be mentioned, express it as part of the major heading or add another subhead.
2. Use parallel phrasing. Do not use a word or phrase for one topic, a sentence for another. Topic, sentence, and paragraph outlines should be consistent in structure throughout.
3. Avoid meaningless headings such as *Introduction*, *Conclusion*, *Reasons*, and *Effects*. If you feel they must appear, add specific explanatory subheads.
4. The first main heading of the outline should not repeat the title of the paper. If the idea expressed in the title logically should appear in the outline, at least rephrase it.
5. Avoid putting into a subhead any matter that should ap-

pear in a larger division; even more important, do not list in a main heading material belonging in a subdivision.

6. Follow conventional uses of indention, symbols, and punctuation.

Study the specimen outlines in this chapter. Note the use of Roman numerals beginning flush left in a topic outline. Observe that capital letters (A,B,C) indicate the first series of subdivisions, and study their indention. If needed, the next series of subdivisions is indicated by Arabic numerals (1,2,3). If still further subdivision is needed, use small letters (a,b,c). Observe that a period follows each numeral or letter and, in sentence and paragraph outlines, each sentence.

Get into the habit of outlining—in your mind or notebook—every assignment you prepare for class, every talk you plan to give, every quiz or examination you are required to take. Bringing order to your study, which outlining is intended to do, cannot fail to increase your grasp of a subject and your grades in it.

26

Discover Your Library

No educational institution lacks a library of some sort. Most educators firmly insist that a library is the heart of any school, college, or institute.

Unfortunately, some students (1) ignore the library available to them or (2) misunderstand its purpose or (3) don't know how to use it intelligently. Ridding yourself of these shortcomings is an immensely important step toward increased satisfaction in educational work and improved grades.

The word *library* comes from the Latin *liber*, meaning "book." A library, however, is more than a collection of books. It is a depository of the written word, yes, but it is also a place for the storage of thought and experience in pictures, manuscripts, tape recordings, microfilm, phonograph records, periodicals, newspapers, and other varieties of information. Thanks to a library, anyone can stand on the shoulders of giant thinkers of the past and present. A good library is a true symbol of civilization.

According to many students, one important reason for attending school—any school—is to make friends. Used sensibly, confidently, and resourcefully, the best and longest-lasting friends any student can make are a library and a dictionary (see Chapter 17). Both will open doors to enormous amounts of personal satisfaction in school and later life. Learning to use and rely on them will lead to a more exciting, less monotonous, far richer existence. Discovering the resources of a good library and a good dictionary is inseparable from the widening of intellectual horizons. Of more immediate concern, their intelligent and regular use will lead to higher grades.

The resources, satisfactions, and pleasures of a public or school library cannot be yours until you learn how to use it sensibly and without wasting time and motion. Also, until you learn what a library really is and how it functions, you may be afraid to tackle it.

Libraries differ widely in size and physical arrangement, but easily understood basic principles apply to the structure and organization of all of them. You can become an intimate friend of your library by getting to know its

1. Physical arrangement
2. Card catalog
3. Periodical indexes
4. Reference books

PHYSICAL ARRANGEMENT

Before losing time through a trial-and-error method of discovering the resources of the library you use, devote a free hour (or several of them) to a tour of its physical arrangement. Your use of a library, any library, will be more efficient if you know the location of the items you are almost certain to use. Also, a tour of the library will uncover stores of information that you may wish to investigate later.

Examine the main reading room, reserved-book room, study alcoves, carrels, reference section, and periodical room. Your particular library may not be arranged to include such divisions, but it will have an equivalent organization, on a smaller or larger scale. You should find out where the desk is located at which books are charged out for home or classroom use, where the card catalog is located, where current magazines and newspapers are filed or racked. Books of fiction (novels and stories) are arranged in most libraries in sections to themselves, shelved alphabetically by author; find out if your library employs this system. Stroll in the room or section where reference books are located and discover the kind and location of books there.

Your library may have available a guide, handbook, or pamphlet that explains its organization and sets forth regulations for its use. If so, examine it carefully. In addition, both your teacher and a librarian will be equipped and eager to answer any reasonable questions you may have about the physical arrangement of the library and the most efficient means of using its resources.

The Card Catalog

A large library contains a vast amount of material of varied kinds. Even a small library has a wealth of sources that will bewilder the outsider. The key to this treasure (or at least its collection of books and bound magazines) is the card catalog. This index to a library consists of 3-by-5 cards filed alphabetically in long trays or drawers and located in a series of filing cabinets. Book information may be found in a card catalog in three ways: (1) by author, (2) by title, (3) by subject.

In most libraries, every nonfiction book is represented by at least three cards, identical except that certain lines giving subject headings and joint author may be typed across the top. If you know the author or the title of a book, you will obtain needed information most easily from an author or title card. If you know the name of neither, consult the subject card for books dealing with the subject about which you are seeking information.

In addition to telling you what books are in the library, the card catalog provides the call number by means of which each book is located on the shelves. Many libraries are arranged so that all (or some) of their books are placed on open shelves easily accessible to readers. If this is the system used in your library, the call number will help you quickly locate the volume you are seeking. In other libraries, the main collection of books is shelved in closed stacks; in order to get a book, you fill out a "call slip" furnished by the library and present it at the Circulation or Loan desk. A library worker will then locate the book by using its call number, and the book will be lent to you.

In every library, books are arranged according to a system, the notational expression of which is the first part of the call number. The two classification systems most commonly used in the United States are the Dewey Decimal classification and the Library of Congress classification. Some knowledge of each is helpful because you probably will use different libraries at different times.

In the Dewey Decimal system, fields of knowledge are arranged in ten groups, including one group for reference or general books. Each major class and each subclass is represented by a three-digit number. Further subdivisions are indicated by numbers actually following a decimal point. On a separate line beneath the Dewey number will be found the author and book number. Books are classified in the Dewey Decimal system as follows:

000–099 General works (encyclopedias, periodicals, and so on)
100–199 Philosophy (psychology, and so on)
200–299 Religion (mythology)

300–399 Social sciences (economics, government, and so on)
400–499 Language (linguistics, dictionaries, and so on)
500–599 Pure science (mathematics, chemistry, and so on)
600–699 Applied science (engineering, aviation, and so on)
700–799 Arts and recreation (painting, music, and so on)
800–899 Literature (poetry, plays, and so on)
900–999 History (travel, 910–919; biography, 920–929)

In the Dewey Decimal system, each book has its own call number. For instance, American literature has the subclassification 810–819. An edition of Longfellow's translation of the *Divine Comedy* has the call number 811 and beneath this the author and book number L86d. The 811 is the Dewey Decimal classification. The L86d is the author and book number; *L* is the first letter of the author's name, and *d* is the first letter of the title.

The Library of Congress classification uses letters of the alphabet followed by other letters or by Arabic numerals. The following are its main classes:

A. General works
B. Philosophy, religion
C. History, auxiliary sciences
D. History, topography (except American)
E., F. American history
G. Geography, anthropology
H. Social sciences
J. Political sciences
K. Law
L. Education
M. Music
N. Fine arts
P. Language and literature
Q. Science
R. Medicine
S. Agriculture, husbandry
T. Technology
U. Military Science
V. Naval science
Z. Bibliography, library science

In this system PS 303–324 is devoted to American poetry, PS 700 on to individual authors, PS 2250–2298 to Henry W. Longfellow. Longfellow's *Evangeline* has the call number PS 2263.

Some libraries use a strictly alphabetical order for filing cards, but most of them follow the rules outlined below.

All libraries file by entry, that is, according to what appears first on the card, whether author, subject, or title. Articles that comprise the first word of a title are ignored; most libraries file letter-by-letter to the end of the word. This means that the title card *The American Way* would be filed in front of the subject card AMERICANISMS, just as all cards beginning with *New York* would be filed in front of cards with *Newark* as the entry word. Libraries that use a system of strictly alphabetical order would, of course, file *-isms* before *way* and *-ark* before *York.* It may be noted that encyclopedias, as well as library catalogs, differ in this fundamental rule. Abbreviations and numerals are filed just as they would be if the words they represent were spelled out.

Books that are *about* an author (considered subject entries and typed in red or in black capitals) are filed after books that are *by* that author.

Author cards having the same surname as the entry word are filed according to the given name; always note carefully the first name, or at least the initials, of an author and the exact title of the book you wish.

When an entry name is the same, all authors by that name precede all subjects, and all subjects come before all titles. Hence, Washington, George (books by), WASHINGTON, GEORGE (books about), *Washington Merry-go-round* (title) are filed in that order.

PERIODICAL INDEXES

Current and recent issues of magazines are often displayed in libraries, sometimes in a periodical room. Older issues of magazines and of some newspapers are normally bound in book form. Some libraries own microfilm records of one or more leading newspapers. To find what you wish in them, consult periodical indexes. These are helpful guides to articles and other items that otherwise might lie buried.

When you consult a periodical index, turn first to the front; here you will find lists of the periodicals indexed and helpful, full instructions for use of the volume.

For example, here are two entries from *Readers' Guide to Periodical Literature* and their meanings:

Author entry: MANCHESTER, Harland
What you should know about flammable fabrics.
Read Digest
90:37–8+ My '67

This entry means that Harland Manchester published an article entitled "What You Should Know about Flammable Fabrics" in the *Reader's Digest* for May 1967. The volume number is 90. The article begins on page 37 and continues on page 38 and later pages.

Subject entry: MARINE painting
Frederick Waugh. America's most popular marine painter.
G. R. Havens IL Am Artist 31:30–7+ Ja '67

An illustrated article on the subject marine painting entitled "Frederick Waugh, America's Most Popular Marine Painter," by G. R. Havens, will be found in volume 31 of *American Artist*, pages 30–37 (continued on later pages of the same issue) of the January 1967 number.

Indexes are of two kinds. *General* indexes list the contents of magazines and a few newspapers of widespread circulation and interest. Unless you are working on some highly specialized and rather unusual subject, a general index, such as the *Readers' Guide to Periodical Literature, Facts on File, The New York Times Index*, or *The Social Sciences and Humanities Index*, probably will meet your needs. *Special* indexes, occasionally more helpful than general ones, restrict themselves to coverage of one particular area. *Agricultural Index, Applied Science and Technology Index, Art Index, Chemical Abstracts, Engineering Index*, and *Psychological Abstracts* are examples of special indexes.

Here is an annotated list of the ten periodical indexes likely to be of most use to you. (If your library does not subscribe to them, consult the librarian about your specific needs and interest. The librarian may be able to make other suggestions or provide adequate substitute material.)

1. *Annual Magazine Subject-Index*, 1907–1949. A subject index, until discontinued, to a selected list—dealing mainly with history, travel, and art—of American and British periodicals and professional or cultural society publications.
2. *Bibliographic Index*, A *Cumulative Bibliography of Bibliographies*, 1937—. A subject index to separately published bibliographies, and to bibliographies included each year in several hundred books and approximately 1500 periodicals.
3. *Public Affairs Information Service Bulletin*, 1915—. A cumulative subject index to current books, pamphlets, periodicals, government documents, and other library material in the fields of economics and public affairs.
4. *Facts on File*, 1940—. A weekly world news digest with cumulative index, including world, national, and foreign affairs, Latin America, finance and economics, art and science, education and religion, sports, obituaries, and other miscellany.
5. *Index to Legal Periodicals*, 1908—. A cumulative subject and author index to articles in law journals.

6. The *Social Sciences and Humanities Index*, formerly the *International Index to Periodicals*, 1907—. A cumulative author and subject index to articles in domestic and foreign periodicals dealing with literature, history, social science, religion, drama, and pure science. It is really a supplement to *Readers' Guide*, below.
7. *The New York Times Index*, 1913—. A cumulative guide to events of national importance by reference to day, page, and column of *The New York Times*. Material is entered by subjects, persons, and organizations. The only index to an American newspaper, it is an indirect guide to other newspapers.
8. *Nineteenth Century Readers' Guide to Periodical Literature*, 1890–1899, with supplementary indexing, 1900–1922, 2 vols.
9. *Poole's Index to Periodical Literature.* 7 vols. An index of articles, by subject only, in American and British periodicals from 1802 to 1906.
10. *Readers' Guide to Periodical Literature*, 1900—. A cumulative index, most useful to the general reader, to over 100 popular and semipopular magazines. Entries are according to author, subject, and fiction title.

Reference Books

Any book can be used for reference, but those that merit the name are condensed, authoritative, conveniently arranged, and up to date. (The preparation of a genuine reference book is expensive in time, money, and effort. It cannot be revised and reprinted often and therefore is not always strictly current.)

In many libraries, reference books are available on shelves open to students or on tables in a special reference section. Your instructor, or the school or reference librarian, can tell you which of the scores of reference books at hand are likely to be most helpful with a particular subject. In addition, if your library has a copy of any of the following titles, examine it carefully for useful, time-saving hints on using reference books:

American Library Association. *Ready Reference Collection.* Chicago: American Library Association, 1962.

Barton, Mary Neill. *Reference Books: A Brief Guide for Students and Other Users of the Library*, 6th ed. Baltimore: Enoch Pratt Free Library, 1966.

Hoffman, Hester R. *Reader's Adviser* and *Bookman's Manual*, 10th ed. New York: R. R. Bowker, 1964.

Murphey, Robert W. *How and Where To Look It Up.* New York: McGraw-Hill, 1958.

Winchell, Constance M. *Guide to Reference Books*, 8th ed. Chicago: American Library Association, 1967. Supplements.

Reference works are so numerous and so varied in content and quality that it would be impossible to discuss all of them. But you should become acquainted with such important works as these:

GENERAL ENCYCLOPEDIAS

Collier's Encyclopedia. 24 vols. Kept up to date with an annual volume, *Collier's Year Book Covering National and International Events.*

Columbia Encyclopedia, 3rd ed.

Columbia–Viking Desk Encyclopedia, 2nd ed.

Encyclopaedia Britannica. 30 vols. Kept up to date with an annual volume, *Britannica Book of the Year, a Record of the March of Events.*

Encyclopedia Americana. 30 vols. Kept up to date with an annual volume, *The Americana Annual, an Encyclopedia of Current Events.*

International Encyclopedia of the Social Sciences. 17 vols.

New International Encyclopedia. 25 vols. Kept up to date with an annual volume, *New International Year Book, a Compendium of the World's Progress.*

Seligman, Edwin R. A., and Alvin Johnson (eds.). *Encyclopaedia of the Social Sciences* (commonly known as ESS). 15 vols. Less comprehensive than the volumes listed above, it deals with many subjects directly and indirectly related to the social sciences.

GENERAL DICTIONARIES

Funk & Wagnalls New Standard Dictionary of the English Language.

Murray, Sir James A. H., *et al.* (eds.). *A New English Dictionary on Historical Principles,* reissued as *The Oxford English Dictionary.* 13 vols. (Commonly referred to as the NED or OED.)

The Random House Dictionary of the English Language.

Webster's New International Dictionary of the English Language.

YEARBOOKS

(These are in addition to the annual yearbooks of the various encyclopedias.)

Annual Register: A Review of Public Events at Home and Abroad (British).

Europa Yearbook. 2 vols. Vol I, Europe; Vol. II, Africa, The Americas, Asia, Australia.

Information Please Almanac. Miscellaneous information in compact form.

International Yearbook and Statesmen's Who's Who. Data on countries and political leaders.

Reader's Digest Almanac and Yearbook. Miscellaneous information.

Statesman's Year-book: Statistical and Historical Annual of the States of the World. Over 100 annual volumes have been published.

United Nations Yearbook.

World Almanac and Book of Facts. Miscellaneous information.

Your library probably has additional encyclopedias, handbooks, and dictionaries. Special reference works are available dealing with subjects such as biography, business and economics, education, drama and the theater, history, language, literature, music and the dance, painting and architecture, philosophy and psychology, religion, and science. Some of these special subject reference books will be useful. Ferret them out. Once again, a good reference book is the place where you should start any research project you have (see Chapter 27).

27

Take Three Steps to Better Papers and Reports

In many courses you are required to prepare papers outside class. Such papers may be assigned as lengthy research projects but more often involve a summary based on reading, a book report, a report on an experiment, or a personal investigation of some sort. Improving the content, form, and appearance of such assignments will obviously better your grades in any course you are taking.

Wholly aside from class assignments, it will help to learn how to prepare reports. In many learning situations, activities require summaries or reports from class secretaries, treasurers, committee chairpersons, and other officers or representatives. Learning to write reports of varied kinds will help you as an official of a civic group, chairman of a management or union committee, supervisory employee in a business firm, and in numerous other roles.

Since most reports are likely to involve research of some kind, you should know what the word really means. It came into our language from an old French word, *cercher*, meaning to seek or search, and the prefix *re-* (again). Research is an intensive search for the purpose of becoming certain.

The essentials of research are as natural as eating and sleeping. On your own, you have gone from one store to another to locate the dress or suit that looked best on you and was the best bargain. You have tried out various restaurants, soft drinks, and movie theaters in what are actually research projects. In a sense, isn't even dating a problem in research?

Preparing a full-length research paper is an involved, tedious operation. Because of their complexity and time requirements, research papers are not so often assigned as formerly they were. The formal research paper should never be undertaken without detailed instruction and advice from your teacher as well as careful study of any of a number of excellent books and pamphlets dealing with the subject. If you are assigned a research paper, do not undertake it lightly and do allow ample time for its preparation.

Because elaborate research reports (or term papers or investigative compositions, as they are also called) have often proved too time-consuming and the results too frequently disappointing, your teachers are likely to assign one or more comparatively short papers and reports. Less involved than full-length research papers, these too require some research and normally involve six steps:

1. Choosing (or being assigned) a subject
2. Analyzing the subject to find out what is involved
3. Investigating it carefully
4. Taking notes on reading or on interviews
5. Preparing an outline
6. Writing and revising

The remainder of this chapter concerns itself with the two kinds of papers you are most likely to be assigned: reports and book reviews.

Reports

A *report* is an account or statement describing in adequate detail an event, situation, or circumstance, usually as the result of observation or inquiry. As a verb, *report* means literally to "carry back" and more generally means to "relate what has been learned by seeing and investigating."

As someone has observed, if you witness a person entering a thicket where you have noticed a reptile and cry "Look out for the snake," you have produced an efficient report. That is, you have clearly, briefly, and effectively conveyed important and useful information on a single topic about which you have become knowledgeable.

Report writing, however, is usually less simple and informal than this warning about a snake. It may involve two or three pages of expository writing or, possibly, many pages bound in a folder containing pictures, diagrams, and charts. Unless you are told otherwise, follow these steps:

1. *Plan and outline the report carefully.*

A good report is one which contains enough accurate and pertinent information to accomplish the job designed—and not one bit more. To ensure adequate but not excess coverage, outline the report before you begin or frame one as you proceed. No satisfactory report was ever written without an outline prepared in advance or developed as the writing progressed (see Chapter 25).

Such a plan for an informal report might cover these questions:

1. Who asked you to study the problem? When? Why?
2. Precisely what is the subject to be reported on?

3. How was the investigation made? (Authorities consulted, people interviewed, places visited, tests made, reading done.)
4. What are the specific results or recommendations?

In a formal or lengthy report, a summary of methods used to obtain information and of results or recommendations comes first. This summary is followed by the main body of the report which discusses these summary points in detail. A list of topics on "Club Conditions in This School" might resemble this:

1. Summary
2. Members of the investigating committee
3. Methods of conducting the survey
4. Number and kinds of clubs investigated
5. Means of selecting club members
6. Activities of the clubs involved in this study
7. Club contributions to the school
8. Clubs and school elections
9. Clubs and the community
10. Effects of clubs on the student body

Not every report must contain mention of each of these items, nor need those points which appear be handled in the exact order indicated. The plan of an effective report is usually dictated by the opening *summary*, an illustration of which follows:

> The purpose of this report is to determine (1) whether the program designed to give new employees an understanding of the products and social significance of the company has actually justified its cost in time and money; and (2) whether changes are needed to improve the program if it is retained.
>
> The investigation has been based on four sources of information: (1) interviews with employees who have completed the program; (2) interviews with supervisory personnel; (3) sta-

tistical comparisons of work efficiency between those who have and have not taken the program; (4) published reports on related programs at four other industrial centers.

The report establishes the value of the program and recommends its continuation. Suggestions for improvement: (1) Top-level executives should contribute more actively to the program through individual interviews with employees and by lectures to groups; (2) greater use of visual-aid material is needed to explain certain complex company operations; (3) the orientation course should be extended by two weeks.

2. *Make your report selective but comprehensive.*

No report reveals everything known about any subject; a good report writer indicates ability as much by what he omits as by what he includes. Nevertheless, no competent reporter regrets collecting more material than he can use; only if he collects more than he needs can he "write from strength" by appearing to have in reserve more than he actually uses.

3. *Make your report objective and direct.*

An investigator who knows what answers he wishes to get and uses data to support his predetermined point of view is neither a competent nor a fair reporter. A report should be approached without personal prejudice; results and recommendations should be based on materials collected and assembled with an open mind. An effective report contains no exaggerations and few superlatives. The reliable report writer presents facts as clearly as possible and phrases recommendations without appealing to emotion.

Each paragraph in a report should begin with a topic sentence. A reader who, after absorbing the opening summary, wishes to examine in detail a particular part of the report should be able to locate that part at once by glancing at topic sentences only.

The writer of a good report comes to each point at once and adds no unnecessary details.

Some reports present opportunities for graphic representation. You do not need to develop professional skill in visual representation, but you should be aware that charts, maps, drawings, graphs, photographs, and diagrams may be helpful. If your report would be aided by the use of illustrative material, discuss the matter with your instructor or consult a reliable reference book on the graphic representation of data.

Book Reviews

Another kind of report—a report on reading—is frequently assigned under the name of "book review." Such a report consists of a description, evaluation, and analysis of a book. Reading and reporting on such a book is expected to be an extension of the course being taken and is designed to supplement or reinforce textbook and classroom instruction.

Many people write book reports that stop short of what is expected. They feel that when they have read a book and given a summary of its contents or a synopsis of its plot, they have done all that is required. Not so. An effective book review answers these three questions:

1. What was the author trying to do?
2. How well did he succeed in his attempt?
3. What value has the attempt?

An answer to the first question should be a discussion of the scope and purpose of the book. What material is covered? What material is stressed? What was the author's apparent purpose in writing the book?

The second question requires comment not so much on material as on manner. What stylistic faults and excellencies does the book possess? Is it convincing, persuasive, dull? Would some readers find the book excellent, others think it inferior? What readers? Why?

The third question may be answered by a discussion of the theme and purpose of the book. Here you may criticize an author for having written a light romance instead of a novel of social significance, or vice versa. But remember: fairness demands that you first evaluate a book in terms of what it is designed to be. Later, if you wish, you may point out the worthiness or unworthiness of the attempt.

There are three different kinds, or methods, of book reviewing. The first is the method of the reporter: the reviewer reports on the book as an item of news. He tells what the book contains, perhaps in the form of a précis or résumé; he tells something of the author and his or her method of handling material. This type of review is not critical. It reports, in some detail, the observable facts about the author and contents of the book and does little else.

Another method, the one most frequently expected by teachers, is that of combining reportorial details with some critical comment. The writer of this kind of review not only reports but also explains, interprets, and evaluates the book in terms of its material, its style, its scope, and its purpose. Such a review is ordinarily composed of about 50 percent summary and 50 percent evaluation.

The third method has been called the "springboard review." This type of criticism deals only slightly with the actual book under consideration; the "reviewer" uses it merely as a convenient starting point from which he launches into a critical essay that ranges far afield. For example, a springboard reviewer, in considering a book on war, may make a few comments about the book and then proceed to a discussion of other books on war, the dominant psychology of war novels, or even to an analysis of the causes of international friction.

The good review is usually a blend of these three methods. It contains some reportorial detail and some critical comment. It also compares and contrasts the book and its author with other similar or dissimilar books and authors, in an attempt to "place" the book and its special contribution.

Writing effective short papers and reports is not an activity that should be left to the last moment (see Chapter 5). A good short report requires you to think straight (see Chapter 6). It requires careful planning and outlining (see Chapter 25). And finally, an effective short paper deserves the best physical appearance you can give it (see Chapters 28 and 29). In other words, a good paper will demand from you just about everything that is covered elsewhere in this book.

28

Write Legibly

What you write and how you write it are all-important, but you should never overlook the effect upon your grades of neatness, legibility, and orderly presentation.

Being human, teachers sometimes give grades higher than deserved to papers that are unusually neat and presentable. Some teachers are likely to assign a low grade to writing that, regardless of its content, is slovenly and hard to read. Penalizing writing that is difficult to decipher and rewarding that which is easily and quickly scanned may seem unfair, but the practice is more widespread than many teachers will admit or are even conscious of.

Neatness alone is not enough to ensure a satisfactory grade on written work. Actually, neatness unaccompanied by solid worth is a "cop out." And yet a sure and positive step toward better grades is providing ideas with the outward form that will guarantee ready communication and a favorable response.

Consider this analogy. At a social gathering your body may be clean, your mind witty, your disposition genial and pleasant.

But what if your clothes need cleaning, pressing, or ironing; your fingernails are filthy; your hair needs soap and a comb? In the eyes of some, your contribution to the gathering—no matter how worthwhile—will be downgraded because of outward appearances.

Yes, by itself, neatness is superficial in both social affairs and schoolwork. But one aspect of neatness, *legibility*, is *not* superficial. In the business world, reports of losses traceable to misread handwriting are common. Prevalent also are damage suits arising from illegible prescriptions and hospital instructions written by physicians and nurses. Nearly everyone in the commercial world is constantly faced with illegible order forms, signatures, and memos. How many times have you puzzled over a letter from a friend, uncertain of what he or she really wrote? How much of your own correspondence is difficult to read?

It will pay to become conscious of the appearance of your handwriting. Have you recently looked at it carefully and critically? Have you ever asked a friend, acquaintance, fellow employee, teacher, or member of your family to point out to you those parts of your script that are hard to read? Even more important, are you aware of your indifferent handwriting but resigned to it? Do you think of it as an unavoidable weakness? Do you take pride in handwriting that you think expresses your personality, your individuality—no matter how illegible it may be?

Don't hurry past these questions. Careful consideration of them can lead to action that will not only raise your course grades but will also give you satisfaction in reaching a worthwhile goal.

This goal should be legibility at a reasonably rapid rate. No teacher expects handwriting on a quiz or test to be as neat and attractive as on papers prepared outside class. But teachers have a right to expect that all written work will be legible, even that done under pressure and within a time limit.

For most people, legibility and speed are enemies. Nearly everyone can write neatly and legibly when the pace is slow.

Nearly everyone's handwriting loses legibility when it is speeded up. Attaining legibility at varying rates of speed requires attention, application, and practice. Here are five suggestions that should help:

1. *Restudy the basic forms of letters of the alphabet.*

At one time, you knew basic forms well. In reading, you still know them. But only when you write slowly are you likely to make them clearly: an *a* that doesn't look something like an *o*, an *i* and *e* that are distinct, an *n* that doesn't resemble a *u* or an *m*, and so forth. In an objective type examination, your examiner may understandably confuse your *G* and *C* or *F* and *E*. If you write numerals that look alike—say *4* and *7*, or *6* and *8*, or *9* and *7*—they need practice, too.

Each of us can cure bad letter and numeral construction by careful, repeated tracing of all letters of the alphabet and the numerals through 9. Concentrate on those you make least clearly. If necessary, study the models in an elementary book on penmanship or those in handwriting you consider worthy of imitation. It may seem beneath your dignity to do this, but only by tracing letters over and over will you learn to make them clearly, whether writing slowly or rapidly. Tracing letters in this fashion will ensure that habits of mind and muscle are firmly fixed.

2. *Hold your pen or pencil correctly.*

If you have it, rid yourself of the childish habit of holding your pen or pencil at the end. The tip of your index finger should be at least half an inch from the end. Thus held, your writing instrument will exert a uniform pressure on paper. Also, this practice will help you to avoid the finger-tensing that often results in cramping and muscle fatigue.

3. *Use a suitable pen or pencil.*

A sharpened pencil moves more evenly and cleanly over paper than does a blunt one. If you use a fountain pen, see that the ink is black or blue-black. The same color of ink should be in your ballpoint. Colored inks may be useful and even desirable in charts, diagrams, maps, and the like, but not in general writing.

4. *Watch your posture.*

It is difficult to write legibly and rapidly when you are slumping in a chair, standing, or lying in bed. Writing must occasionally be done when you are in an awkward position. Normally, you should sit comfortably upright with paper squarely in front of you (if you are right-handed) and your feet, both of them, on the floor. Unless you have vision problems, your eyes should be at least one foot from the paper.

5. *Watch the overall appearance of your handwriting.*

Several flaws can mar the general pattern of your writing. Running words too closely together is such a flaw. Lines should not be written without adequate space between them. Some writers sprawl their words over a page, covering it with only a portion of the number that would appear in a neat, compact style of handwriting. Irregularity in the size of letters can mar a pattern. Writing uphill or down is an immature interference with the principle that lines should move evenly from left to right. The consecutive letters in a word should be joined; failure to connect them results in a jagged appearance. Watch what you're doing and *keep watching.*

Typewriting

Typescript is more legible than handwriting. With rare exceptions, it is neater and more attractive. In addition, one can usually detect errors more easily in typescript than in handwriting. In other words, whenever it is possible to type your written work, do so.

If you don't know how to type, learning might be an excellent investment of time and money. Many schools provide courses in typing. Commercial courses are not necessarily time-consuming or expensive. Self-teaching books are also available. In fact, one can become fairly expert in the "hunt and peck" system of typing without formal instruction of any kind. Nevertheless, for anyone who plans to do much writing or thinks that it is a useful skill, touch typing is important. It is a saver of time, energy, and money. It will also help improve grades.

The heart of touch typing is learning (knowing) the correct finger to use for each letter, figure, or mark on the typewriter keyboard. Correct fingering is essential for speed and accuracy. Whether you type properly or "hunt and peck," remember always to

1. Strike the keys with the balls of your fingers. Don't pound. Each impression should be a quick tap applied with uniform pressure.
2. Keep your arms away from the machine. Especially, do not rest your wrists on the typewriter frame.
3. Curve your fingers; don't curl them.
4. Always use reasonably good (heavy) bond paper.
5. Don't overwork a typewriter ribbon. Faint or smudged typescript is almost as upsetting to a reader as slovenly handwriting.

In improving the legibility and rapidity of your handwriting and the skill of your typing, remember that writing is a visual record of thought. It is made by prescribed, controlled movements of a hand-controlled instrument: pen, pencil, or typewriter. One commentator has referred to writing as "frozen motion." Since writing cannot be unfrozen once it is set down, it should be as neat and attractive as one can make it. This is a step toward better grades that everyone can take without much fuss, bother, or mental exertion.

29

Revise and Proofread Everything You Write

"There is no such thing as good writing; there is only good re-writing." Many persons have objected to this statement. They will mention an occasion when they really "got going" and turned out an effective first, last, and only draft. Or they will say, "I wrote this paper in an hour and got a C grade on it: here's one which took about four hours and was marked D." Or they will recall that Shakespeare never "blotted a line" or that Sir Walter Scott or O. Henry or this and that writer never rewrote his material.

The fact is that the writer of a good "hour" paper probably had composed it in his or her mind many times before setting it down on paper. It had been thought through; it was written "on the hoof," while walking, eating, dressing, even bathing. The "quickly written" paper was not quickly written at all, even though it was put on paper rapidly.

Not even a professional writer can plan, write, and proof-read all at one time. A naïve and inexperienced person tends to think that a writer just writes, the words pouring out. Yet most skilled writers have testified that writing is laborious, time-consuming work. If an experienced professional can get only a few hundred words on paper during a full working day, he may feel encouraged and happy. Consider this comment from the late John Steinbeck, a Nobel Prize winner:

> Many years of preparation preceded the writing of *Grapes of Wrath.* I wrote it in one hundred days, but the preparation, false starts, and wasted motion took two and a half years. The actual writing is the last process.

In commenting on the rewriting that went into his novel *The Sound and the Fury*, William Faulkner said simply, "I wrote it five separate times." Truman Capote, author of many works of fiction and nonfiction including *In Cold Blood*, has said of all his work: "I write my first version in pencil. Then I do a complete revision, also in longhand. I think of myself as a stylist, and stylists can become notoriously obsessed with the placing of a comma, the weight of a semicolon. Obsessions of this sort, and the time I take over them, irritate me beyond endurance."

Want more proof? Thornton Wilder, the eminent dramatist and novelist, once said, "My wastepaper basket is filled with works that went a quarter through. . . . I forget which of the great sonneteers said 'One line in the fourteen comes from the ceiling, the others have to be adjusted around it.' But it's the joint and cement between those passages that take a great deal of rewriting. . . . Each sentence is a skeleton accompanied by enormous activity of rejection."

When asked about rewriting, short-story writer Frank O'Connor replied that he did so "endlessly, endlessly, endlessly." Then he added, "And I keep on rewriting after something is published."

Alberto Moravia, a widely respected and popular Italian writer, commented: "Each book is worked over several times. I like to compare my method with that of painters centuries ago, proceeding from layer to layer. The first draft is quite crude, by no means finished. After that, I rewrite it many times—apply as many layers—as I feel to be necessary."

Are you still unconvinced that all writing, even that of professional craftsmen, requires revision? Then listen to this from James Thurber when asked "Is the act of writing easy for you?" His response: "It's mostly a question of rewriting. It's part of a constant attempt to make the finished version smooth, to make it seem effortless. A story I've been working on was rewritten fifteen complete times. There must have been 240,000 words in all. I must have spent 2000 hours working on it. Yet the finished version is only 20,000 words." And when asked "Then it's rare that your work comes out right the first time?" Mr. Thurber replied, "Well, my wife took a look at a first version and said 'That's high school stuff.' I had to tell her to wait until the seventh draft."

Such comments make writing seem like hard work. Well, it is. But those unwilling to revise and rewrite are skipping a major step toward becoming better writers and getting better grades. You may not wish to go to the lengths mentioned here, but some revision and rewriting are essential steps toward making any composition of whatever kind more effective and appealing.

If this advice seems grim, then relax over this amusing comment by Jonathan Swift:

> Blot out, correct, insert, refine,
> Enlarge, diminish, interline;
> Be mindful, when invention fails,
> To scratch your head and bite your nails.

If time permits (and usually it does if you follow the advice given in Chapter 5), revise or rewrite at least some parts of every paper you prepare for any course, any lengthy examination you take, and any important letter you write.

Three kinds of alteration are possible when you revise a paper. You can *substitute*, you can *delete*, and you can *add*. When your reasons for making such changes are considered, certain subdivisions appear.

One such subdivision consists of asking questions like these:

(1) Have I chosen a suitable subject and narrowed it so that in the number of words I have at my disposal I can provide a clear and reasonably complete account of what my reader expects or has a right to expect? (2) Have I followed an orderly plan in writing, working from either a mental or written outline? Have I divided the treatment into related parts and written at least one paragraph on each? (3) Is each of my paragraphs adequate in material, unified in substance, correctly proportioned?

Still another group of alterations consists of efforts to achieve greater accuracy of expression, or more clarity, so as to drive home more forcefully to a reader a particular point, idea, mood, or impression. In this sort of revision, you check and recheck your choice of words; you revise the word order and structure of a sentence or group of sentences; you alter a figure of speech to make an image sharper or clearer; you add a bit of dialogue or an incident or anecdote to reinforce an idea; you remove a section that seems stale and ineffective; you alter the position of sentences within paragraphs or the order of paragraphs in the entire paper.

Consider this small example of revision. A teacher asked students to write a paragraph with this topic sentence: "Lying is bad policy." One student wrote:

> Lying is bad policy. When you tell one lie, you usually have to tell a dozen more to cover up the first one. Even when you try your best to keep from getting caught, you usually wind up red-faced or red-handed. Sometimes the penalty for telling a lie can be severe. Telling the truth may hurt, but it's the only sure way to avoid trouble.

The instructor commented that the paragraph was free from grammatical errors but that it was dull and repetitious. The writer improved it greatly in this revision:

Lying is bad policy. A friend of mine applied for a summer job last year and told a lie about his previous experience when he filed his application. A week after he had started work, his supervisor discovered my friend's claim was false and fired him instantly. My friend not only lost his job, but he couldn't bear to explain what had really happened. Furthermore, it was then too late to get another job and he was miserable all summer long. Now he knows, as I do, that lying is a bad and foolish policy.

Proofreading

When we read, we usually see merely the outlines, or shells, of words. Only poor readers need to see individual letters as such; most of us comprehend words and even groups of words at a glance (see Chapters 7 and 8). But have you ever noticed how much easier it is for you to detect errors in someone else's writing than in your own? This may be because in reading someone else's writing you are looking for mistakes. Or it may be that you look more carefully at the writing of someone else than at your own because you are unfamiliar with it and have to focus more sharply in order to comprehend. You already "know" what you yourself are saying.

Whatever the reason for closer scrutiny, in proofreading we narrow the range of our vision and thereby pick up mistakes hitherto unnoticed. In short, we detect careless errors not by reading but by proofreading.

Much of the effectiveness of proofreading depends upon the spread of your vision. The following triangle will show you how wide your vision (sight spread) is. Look at the top of the triangle and then down. How far down can you go and still identify each letter in each line at a single glance? Your central vision is as wide as the line above the one where you cannot identify each letter without moving your eyes at all.

a
a r
a r d
a r d c
a r d c f
a r d c f g
a r d c f g x
a r d c f g x y
a r d c f g x y z
a r d c f g x y z p
a r d c f g x y z p w

People differ in their range of vision as they do in nearly everything else. But many people have difficulty in identifying more than six letters at a single glance. Some have a span of vision embracing only three or four letters. Whatever your span, you should not try to exceed it when you are carefully checking for errors. If you do, you are reading—perhaps with excellent understanding—but you are not proofreading.

Only proofreading will enable you to eliminate errors caused not by ignorance or stupidity but by carelessness.

In trying to improve your grades, make your written work as error-free as your mind, hand, and sight can make it. Thoughtful revision and careful proofreading of every page you submit in any class are major steps toward that goal.

30

Improve Your Test-taking Methods

Tests are a part of life. There is no escaping them. You face a test of one sort or another nearly all the time, whether it be a few brief questions intended to check on a reading assignment or a two-hour essay examination designed to evaluate a semester's work. College entrance examinations are used to determine readiness for college, admission to the school of one's choice, scholarship eligibility, and advanced standing. Outside school, one takes tests used by employers to evaluate skills necessary for various types of jobs. Nearly all of us continue to take tests all our lives.

Obviously, study is the best preparation for most tests. Many tests, however, determine general knowledge and ability. Detailed study of specific subject matter is impossible. But you can prepare for every test by acquainting yourself with the kinds of questions that are asked.

Before taking any quiz or exam, try to find out from your instructor, or from students who have taken the course before, answers to questions such as these:

1. What will the test cover?
2. How long will it be?
3. Will the test require writing or will it be true–false, multiple-choice, or some other type that can be scored by electronic test-scoring equipment?
4. Will there be a penalty for wrong answers?
5. What weight will be given to accuracy and fullness of answers as contrasted with the form, appearance, and style of any writing required?

When taking a test, if you don't know the material involved, there is little you can do to disguise this. And yet you can do much to weaken your performance. In an excellent guide, *The Effective Student* (Harper & Row, 1966), Dr. H. Chandler Elliott provides these suggestions for failing a test even when one knows the answers:

1. Arrive in a daze due to an (ineffectual) attempt to "cover" the whole course during the night. Your noble efforts will placate the Powers Above, whatever the effect on the examiner.
2. Try to counteract the daze by extra coffee, or by pep pills. This will make you feel awfully clever, however scrambled your presentation.
3. Scan the questions in a flash. If you do misread, your answer will be brilliant enough to rate full credit anyway.
4. Plunge straight ahead without plan or schedule, relying on your unerring instinct. If you run short at the end, write "No more time!" and the examiner will pro-rate what you have done.
5. Don't take instructions seriously; for example, if a diagram is required, give three pages of writing instead. You do it so much better, and the poor, stupid examiner will not know the difference.
6. Write with such frantic speed as to be illegible (a faint pencil helps here). The examiner will assume you are correct on points that he cannot read.

7. On objective, short-answer examinations, make A's that look like H's, C's like G's, 7's like 9's, V's like II's, and so on. Obviously your answer must be right, so anyone can see that you mean A, 7, or whatnot.
8. Spend the time saved by the foregoing techniques using long-winded flowery phrases, digressing and padding. This impresses an examiner far more than a few extra facts.
9. Put an addition to some question at the back, especially after some blank, unnumbered pages. A reader will instinctively realize that you know more than just the first part.
10. Leave out part of a question. You are too rushed to attend to such details.
11. Do not sign your paper. The examiner will rather enjoy a little break from routine, trying to identify it.

Suggestions for taking tests sensibly and effectively include these:

1. Carefully read all questions and instructions before beginning to write. (This suggestion will not apply to all types of standardized, objective tests and examinations.)
2. Budget your time. Follow a thought-out schedule carefully. Leave a margin of safety.
3. Write as clearly and legibly as you can.
4. Look over the test upon completion. Correct errors; check to make sure that nothing is omitted; add afterthoughts of importance.

The remainder of this chapter explains some of the kinds of questions that often appear on tests of general knowledge.

Vocabulary Questions

As a general rule, the larger one's vocabulary, the greater an individual's knowledge. There is a direct relationship between the size of your vocabulary and the amount of knowledge you possess (see Chapter 18). Consequently, questions dealing with vocabulary are commonly used on most tests of general ability.

Questions on vocabulary will require you to (1) match listed words with correct definitions; (2) choose from several listed definitions; (3) choose synonyms; (4) select antonyms; (5) complete analogies; (6) choose words in context. If such requirements seem formidable—and they are—procure one of the numerous paperbound manuals designed to familiarize you with such tests and to provide training in taking them.

ESSAY QUESTIONS

No type of test or examination question frightens most people so much as an essay question. Nearly everyone would rather take objective tests than be faced with questions that demand lengthy answers in intelligible prose.

Essay questions, however, are necessary because they test for the type of information that objective questions tend to ignore. An essay question enables the tester to determine a student's ability to put facts into perspective, to generalize from the data he has assembled, and to draw subjective conclusions from the content of his study. The essay question is also used to measure how well one is able to communicate in writing.

You should approach an essay question with the same care that you give any written assignment. Read the question carefully. Determine exactly what it is the question seeks to discover and the general type of information the answer requires. It is also good practice to sketch out an outline before you begin to write. The preliminary steps in answering an essay question are as important as they are in planning a formal composition.

Perhaps the most difficult step in an essay answer is the framing of the first sentence of the first paragraph. It is frequently possible to restate the central part of the question as the opening sentence. Note the following question:

> In a famous definition of the tragic hero, Aristotle pointed out that he was a man who was not preeminently virtuous or just, but one who came to his tragic end not through some essential lack of goodness but through some error of judgment. How well do you feel that Shakespeare's Julius Caesar measures up or fails to measure up to Aristotle's definition? Use incidents from the play to support your judgment.

Depending upon your judgment, the central part of the question might be expressed as the first sentence of your answer as follows: Caesar fits (or does not fit) perfectly Aristotle's definition of the tragic hero.

Some essay questions merely require you to provide factual data. Most, however, demand that you come to a conclusion or formulate a judgment based upon your study; you must see to it that your conclusions are concretely supported by pertinent facts and examples. Moreover, the relationships between your supporting facts and your conclusion must be evident. Note that the sample question above directs the student to support his answer by citing incidents from *Julius Caesar*.

For example, you may write that Caesar's judgment was affected by his vanity and pride. In an essay answer, such a statement should be supported by specific mention of instances where Caesar is boastful, where he denies that he is ever afraid of anything. You know that fear is a basic human emotion and you might point out that, in his denial of fear, Caesar is actually denying his own humanity. Your conclusion is that his confidence in his superiority over all other men warped his judgment and was thus a major cause of his downfall.

Or you may feel that Caesar's errors of judgment resulted from rashness and imprudence in not paying attention to warnings that might have saved his life. You should cite one or more instances in which Caesar ignores the superstitions and traditions in which he firmly believes but rashly overlooks when tempted by the offer of a crown.

On the other hand, you may feel that Caesar does not really fit Aristotle's definition of the tragic hero at all. It may seem to you that in spite of his pride, vanity, rashness, and ruthless ambition, Caesar is actually a noble figure and that others, not he, are responsible for the tragedy that occurs. If this is your belief, then you should give examples of, for instance, the raw courage and spiritual power that made him a magnificent figure. You might point out that at the end of the play Brutus himself speaks of the triumph of Caesar's spirit. Caesar's body is destroyed, but his spirit lives on.

Whatever your approach, your answer should consist of a conclusion, or series of conclusions, based on examples and citations that set forth precisely what you are trying to communicate.

Little relationship exists between the length of an answer and its worth. Common sense indicates that there is merit in brevity. Many students have a tendency to expand their essay answers, believing that those who evaluate them will be favorably disposed by bulk. On the contrary, those who must read essay answers are impressed by pertinent material economically expressed.

Final Word

Material in this chapter should provide helpful suggestions for taking tests and examinations involving varied kinds of subject matter. But no one should ever forget that each of us is likely to make three serious errors while being examined·

1. We panic
2. We are careless
3. We don't think

Panic may be a greater cause of lower test grades than poor preparation, carelessness, or ignorance. Everyone is, or should be, somewhat tense (or at least actively alert) before an examination, but actual fear can damage, if not paralyze, one's memory, mind, and even physical ability to write and speak. Panic is always irrational, self-made, and self-defeating. We know this only too well from past experiences. But it is silly only to say "Fear is bad. Get rid of it." What one can do is enter an examination room physically rested, as well prepared as possible, and with a firm determination to do one's best. It also helps not to worry about results—at least until after the test has been completed. If you flatly refuse to project results, your confidence will increase and your performance will improve.

Carelessness is a second major cause of poor test performance. After any examination, one can hear students saying, "I knew that, but I read the question wrong" or "But I thought the question was. . . ." It is carelessness when you miss the key words in questions. It is carelessness to read only the first few words in a question, assume what is wanted, and start writing. It is carelessness to "explain" when the question asks you to "list." It is carelessness to mention a half-dozen when asked to give a detailed explanation of *one* result. It is carelessness to copy the wrong number from your scratch paper.

Careless students do not proofread their papers and thus fail to notice errors they could easily correct. (Everyone makes mistakes in writing—especially under pressure—careless, hurried mistakes that lower grades.) It is a good practice never to turn in a test paper until you have checked it. If time is short, it may be better to leave a question unanswered in favor of correcting the answers that you do submit.

Thinking is hard work at any time (see Chapter 6). It is especially hard to do during the rush and pressure of an examination. You may think all you have to do is get on paper what you think you know, with no time wasted.

Using your head, however, is never more important than when taking a test. Some examinations do call for "facts" more than "thoughts," but even giving "just facts" requires careful thought as well as that rare and valuable commodity, common sense. It is also well to remember that as you proceed with your education, you will encounter tests that demand thought, analysis, interpretation, and judgment more than factual information. Even now, your teacher would prefer you to be a thinking person rather than an automaton and "writing fool."